The
Spider
Goddess

The Spider Goddess

Edited and compiled
by Asenath Mason

Temple of Ascending Flame

2022

List of Contents

Introduction

Asenath Mason

This book is dedicated to the Spider Goddess. What exactly does it mean, though? In the Draconian/Typhonian Tradition, the Spider Goddess is the Queen of Space and the Weaver of the Web in the Void. Her role and attributes are much more complex than what we know about her from ancient mythologies, where this archetype is known under such names as Arachne, Uttu, Anansi, the Spider Woman, Māyā, and many others. In Qliphothic Qabalah, she is the queen of dark labyrinths beneath the Cosmic Tree. Her web extends across the Void, bridging the gulf between the Dayside and the Nightside, waking and dreaming, the conscious and the unconscious. Her power is magical venom, which is deadly to mundane consciousness, but essential in the formula of initiation as it triggers the process of transformation through the inner alchemy of the mind. She is also the Weaver of Fate, and the spider as a symbol stands for the art of manipulation of destinies and the ability to maintain balance between past and future, spiritual and physical, creation and destruction. As the Dark Initiatrix, she shows us how to gaze through the veil of illusion and access the Web of Fates, how to change and manipulate it at its roots, and by invoking her essence and absorbing her venom we ourselves acquire the power to weave it, thus becoming the true center of the universe and the very root of all manifestation.

These faces of the Spider Goddess and many more are explored in this book. Like other anthologies by the Temple of Ascending Flame, it contains a unique view of the Spider Current, accessed and presented from the perspective of the Draconian Initiate. It is meant for other Draconian practitioners, but it also contains information that will be of interest to anyone who wants to explore the mysteries of the spider in general. What do these mysteries entail? For this we have to look at the spider itself and the symbolism that has been attached to it by various cultures over the ages.

From the simple meaning, which involves the image of the spider weaving the web as a metaphor for us weaving the threads of our life, to more complex interpretation of the spider gnosis, which includes deep aspects of Qliphothic magic, we can say a lot about spiders. First of all, the spider is a symbol of mystery, as well as creation versus destruction. In many mythologies, it represents fate, and the many threads in the web correspond to multiple life choices that we make to bring ourselves closer to fulfillment of our destiny. The spider is also a predator, with the female eating the male after the copulation, typifying the fierce and ruthless nature of the Spider Current. All of it is contemplated while discussing the spider symbolism. Let us then take a closer look at the leading motifs in the gnosis of the spider, and see what exactly we are dealing with in this book.

First of all, let us focus on the primary symbol that comes to our mind whenever we think of spiders - the web. The spider's web involves many threads arranged in intricate and often beautiful patterns. It is enchanting to look at, and if you have not seen a spider web covered with the morning dew, reflecting the first rays of the sun, you have missed one of the most amazing views in the world. The spider weaves its web from the center to the outer edges, which is often compared to us constructing our life by making choices, taking decisions, and following certain paths out of many opportunities that are presented to us by the universe. The spider web is therefore a symbol of creation and growth, evolution and multiplicity of choices and possibilities. In this interpretation, the spider itself typifies an individual standing in the middle of the web, aware of the choices and options he/she has and looking at them from the perspective of the center. This helps us see our actions and decisions as far-reaching tools by which we can shape our life and give it the meaning we want. By contemplating the web, we are no longer blind to the consequences of our actions, but we can see the possible outcomes of our decisions in the long run.

On the other hand, the primary function of the web is to be a trap. It is through it that the spider lures its prey to feast on it later. Once we are caught in the web, we are stuck and unable to move further. Our energies are slowly drained until there is nothing left, and we become passive observers of our life instead being of masters of our destiny, like a fly trapped in the web versus the spider moving through it freely. Therefore, the spider reminds us to take control of our life and be mindful of our actions and choices, as everything we do can either serve us or enslave us. In Hinduism, the spider web is associated with Māyā, "illusion" - the belief that the world is not what it seems and we can only perceive what is on the surface but the true reality is hidden from us. By working with the Spider Goddess, we learn to look through this illusion and access the very roots of reality, which are also the roots of all creation itself.

The symbolism of the spider's web and the spider in general is full of all kinds of ambiguities. In some cultures, the appearance of the spider web in the house is a bad sign, and sometimes it is even an omen that someone is about to die.

In others, a spider weaving its web in the corner of the room is considered a sign of good luck, prosperity, and the spider's presence is welcome. In ancient Greece, it was believed that sleeping under a spider's web triggers dreams about the future and reveals the truth about the sleeping person. It was a form of an oracle, and the same idea is found in many other cultures across the ancient world. Today we either fear spiders or tolerate them, and some people even have them as their pets, but we rarely think about their spiritual symbolism. By working with the Spider Current, we can change that and gain a better understanding of what it means to "be a spider" or how we can use the web as a metaphor for our personal development. There are many things to be learned from the Spider Goddess, and contemplating her web is only one of many aspects of her multidimensional gnosis.

Associations of the spider with the concept of fate are encountered in many mythologies where human life is seen as a thread spun by a goddess or a group of goddesses. The Greek Moirai, the Norns from the Scandinavian lore, the Roman Parcae - these are the most prominent examples of the Divine Feminine being in charge of human destiny. Among the Moirai, we encounter Clotho (the Spinner), who spins the thread of an individual's life, Lachesis (the Alotter), who dispenses it, and Atropos (the Inflexible), who cuts it when the person's time is due. This is different than the thread of Arachne, though, because here it is linear and the person has no influence over the course of one's life. Arachne is the spider in the center of the web, and her Web of Fates is not linear but cyclic - everything in it is interconnected, and each time we arrive at a crossing of the threads, we have more than just one possibility to act and shape our life. Arachne makes us aware of the choices we make throughout our lives and the way they affect us, as well as their influence on others. In this sense, the spider web can be seen as a symbol of our existence and how we choose to live it. On the surface, we do not always know where the thread will take us or how things will go for us, but when we look at our life from the perspective of the center, through the eyes of the spider, we are able to see how all these patterns interconnect, which gives us a better understanding of what choices we should make to arrive where we want to be. This is the art of manipulating fate and making it work for us, instead of being a passive observer ruled by our "destiny."

The motif of self-knowledge achieved through exploration of the Web of Fates is a recurring concept in working with the Spider Current. The web can be seen in the literal meaning of this word, but many practitioners see it, for example, as a tree with branches leading to various aspects of the Self or as a labyrinth with many doors and rooms. These doors open access to self-knowledge, hidden messages, inner insights, and all kinds of unconscious material that can be revealed by working with the Spider Goddess. Sometimes these places or concepts refer to destiny, showing the past, present and future and how they are all connected. Other times they reveal the present aspects of life, magical path, or simply knowledge of ourselves. Some practitioners see them as particular aspects of their initiatory path, or tests and challenges that they are facing or are still about to face. Others experience the Web of the Spider Goddess in a cosmic sense, connecting the whole universe with its planets, stars, celestial objects, people, places, and so on. The Web of Fates encompasses everything and stretches through all planes and dimensions, bridging the manifest world with the unmanifest, the conscious and the unconscious, the known with the unknown.

The spider is a creator. It spins its web across an empty space, which is often seen as typifying creativity as well as fertility. It is therefore a symbol loaded with positive meanings. Its eight legs reflect the symbolism of the number eight, which is connected with balance and symmetry. It is also reminiscent in its shape of the infinity symbol, which typifies the cyclic nature of the universe, evolution and the pattern of birth-death-rebirth. At the same time, many people are afraid of spiders, seeing them as predators and monsters. This has spiritual connotations, too. The spider is a lunar animal, and therefore it is associated with the Divine Feminine in her dark aspect. It is Arachne, but it is also Lilith, whose essence is so venomous that a drop of it can kill the population of an entire town. The Spider Goddess is an ambiguous figure as well. Just like a female spider eating the male during or after copulation, the Spider Goddess can devour us if she decides we do not have what it takes to walk her path. In mythologies we meet her in many different disguises. She can be a crone, like the Spider Grandmother, who is the wise woman, the initiatrix, the earth goddess, and the guardian of the mysteries of the dark moon. In this sense, she represents the Shadow and the dark side of the Self, the principle that absorbs and devours everything. Therefore, while working with her, we are often faced with the vision of being consumed by her or her children, wrapped in her cocoon for the purpose of self-transformation, or being exposed to her venom that dissolves everything and makes place for new things to rise. This venomous aspect of Arachne is as common as her positive facets, and her energy can often be seen as green, toxic, and venomous, acting as poison within the Initiate's consciousness.

On the other hand, Arachne in the original myth was a beautiful maiden, and this aspect is reflected in the Spider Goddess as well. Sometimes she reveals herself to us in her sexual aspect, seducing the Initiate of her path and leading us to communion through works of eroto-comatose gnosis. In this manifestation, she is often compared to Lilith, who possesses a spider aspect as well, which we meet when we encounter her as the Dark Goddess of Sitra Ahra, sending out her venomous *kalas* throughout the entire Tree of Qliphoth. Most often, however, Arachne manifests in her spider form. She is silver or black, giant, and standing in the center of her web. When she assumes a human form, she has long black hair and shining eyes, and she is surrounded by a toxic green aura. Some practitioners also encounter her as a half-woman half-spider. She spins her web in the center of the universe, its threads forming a network connecting various places and people and leading us to self-discovery and self-realization.

Spiders and spider deities are encountered worldwide, and there is hardly a part of the world where legends and myths would not involve them or attach to them any special meaning. We have already mentioned some of them. The others will be described on the pages of this anthology. Among the most popular spider characters, we can mention the Greek Arachne and Ariadne, the Spider Woman or Spider Grandmother of the Native American folklore, the Sumerian goddess Uttu, or the African Anansi. Even some of the deities we would normally not associate with spiders are sometimes believed to have spider features or to be connected to spiders in some way. The Hebrew Lilith, the Babylonian Ishtar, the Celtic Arianrhod, or the Roman Minerva - are all figures associated with the spider gnosis. Among the less known spider figures, we can mention Nareau, the Lord Spider of Oceania, the Tsuchigumo and the Jorōgumo in Japan, or the Areop-Enap of Micronesia. In occultism, we sometimes encounter entities with spider features, reflecting the nature of the Spider Current, just like the Goetic Bael, for instance, whose spider legs represent the connection to the spider-consciousness and denote the primordial nature of the spirit.

Today, we can see the influence of fascination with the spider symbolism in such characters of popular culture as the Spiderman or the Black Widow, as well as in many other depictions in books, movies and video games. Finally, the motif of spinning the web across the space, connecting various objects and people together is also seen as an analogy for the Internet, or World Wide Web, which is often seen as the most powerful manifestation of the Spider Goddess in the modern world. She is, therefore, around us all the time. Even now, as you read this book, other people may be reading it in other parts of the world, thus making a subtle connection between all of you, like in a spider's web. Spider gnosis is a fascinating domain to explore, and we hope that this anthology will encourage you to pursue it further. At the end of this book you will find the list of resources recommended to study the Spider Current that we have found interesting and relevant to our work with Arachne. Also, if you have any questions about the articles included here, feel free to reach out to the authors - their contact information is included in the contributor's list. We hope that all this information will bring you many powerful and amazing encounters with the Spider Goddess!

Our Lady of Silk and Space

Denerah Erzebet

Introduction

Creation - whether observed as the "work of God" or the result of human effort - proceeds through the execution of several mechanisms and a single *substance* currently operating across natural, mental, and spiritual phenomena. These principles are the foundation of esoteric traditions such as the Hermetic Qabalah wherein "correspondence" reestablishes the true link between heaven and earth, through the operation of *mentality* (defined herein as the faculties of thought, imagination, reason, and dreaming variously applied in the *re-membering* of primordial wisdom).

Remembering, or Initiation, is the sum-total of *experience* engaged in the modification of energy in both time and space. In other words, the manifestation of Something (Identity) from the primordial Anything (Chaos). Likewise, the adept must at times restore or *return* forms to their archetypal essence - only thus will he realize the twin-channels of creativity as *going* between Emanation and Embodiment, Abstract to Phenomenal - *again and again as always!*

Eventually, the magician will stand *as some center* around which the immortal beloved (goddess) invites him to join her dance, to embrace the myriad forms his life will assume. Together, they weave an intricate web of combined experience - all spun from the nameless substratum upon which Life makes itself known.

All of this is embodied in the Spider, in its biological and mythical representations. Her limbs extend in all directions, as she weaves spiritual ideas into material forms, embodying the horizontal and vertical channels of creation: Spirit and Substance.

In this essay, we will explore the Spider as one of three principles employed in all true works of magic, being nothing more than the manifestation of *inspired willpower on behalf of one's personal deity - the Immortal Beloved.*

Naturally, her role must be understood in relation to her sibling-archetypes; leading us to consider the Three Paths of Draconian magic held within the secret tunnels beneath the Temple of Ascending Flame. This trinity forms an interlocking triangle wherein all intentions come forth, in time.

1.
The Three Paths: Serpent - Spider - Siren

Since the publication of *VOVIN,* further explorations were carried out in the astral temple, particularly within the "secret chamber" described in Chapter 4 of that same book.

I must confess that this undertaking was unintentional, even as a long-standing member of the Temple of Ascending Flame. I stood on the threshold of the underground chamber several times, in dreaming, without being granted access beyond. Only under the auspicious gaze of the Dragon, during one of the Temple's inner projects, was I admitted and initiated into the threefold path.

Seeing as the Temple is not a secret nor a hierarchy-based "order," neither is this triple essence. In fact, the Three Paths I am about to describe are open to all Draconian sorcerers who channel the current with sincerity and dedication. While the Temple initiates can certainly enhance their ascent therewith, solitary practitioners can equally embrace this triple-soul.

In fact, the Draconian Trinity is an archetypal representation of the microcosmic faculties within us all, in the same way that Hecate's faces of maiden-mother-crone are personifications of human life from pure enchantment (innocence), to creativity (adulthood) growing into ageless wisdom (maturity).

The three paths can also be approached in spiritual ways, for personal growth and through invocation of their ministering deities.

The trinity was shown as follows:

1) The Way of the Serpent (Lucifer-Samael)
2) The Way of the Spider (Leviathan-Arachne/The Spider Queen)
3) The Way of the Siren (Lilith-Naamah)

As readers will notice, each principle is informed by a pair of patron deities, with apparent-emphasis placed on Lucifer and Lilith as polarized consorts (god and goddess/masculine and feminine). In the center, but likewise in *the background,* Leviathan empowers their work as the cosmic dragon itself.

In other words, distinct realities are brought together through conscious manipulation (or harmonization) of the "blood of the Dragon, primal source of all creation."

The Spider, sharing a similar function, reveals herself as the hidden nature of the path bearing its name. Likewise, Samael and Naamah present themselves as *other aspects* of the aforementioned couple, typically in darker, violent form. (Note: Contrast Lucifer's role of Light-Bearer with Samael's intoxicating poison administered to erode the stronghold of Reason. Similarly, Lilith prevails as Great Mother while her impetuous daughter, Naamah, shows far less consideration for the adept's comfort during sexual initiations.)

As such, these darker consorts embody the harsh conflict at the root of earthly life. Only the Spider Queen's unforgiving logic can bind chaos in her eternal web!

We become the Spider Goddess through self-criticism, and through the virtues of *responsibility, discipline, judgement, and integrity.*

She also extends to include both cosmos and the dancing couple locked in creative ecstasy!

2.
The Personal Thread

In the microcosm, we observe three crucial methods for effective sorcery. Eastern teaching identifies them as *Mantra, Yantra,* and *Mudra.* These generally refer to vocalized sounds, symbols, and gestures. Typically, Western Traditions employ them in the form of incantations, sigils, and ceremonial magic (i.e. structured and symbolically consistent rituals).

They correspond to the paths as follows:

1) Mantra or incantation, as the conscious formulation of Intent channels Lucifer's illumination, freedom, and consciousness. It is both the serpent in Eden, and the semblance of sound to undulate (vibrate) through space.
2) Yantra evokes the use of glamor, illusion, and enchantment, belonging to the Lilith's seductive and bewitching character.
3) Mudra is the cohesive structure of the full rite itself, wherein previous elements are consistently upheld for a specific purpose at any given time; thus binding the various elements of one's life into a singular, grand vision composed of dynamic, yet harmonious, parts.

The Spider not only occupies itself with organizing rituals, but also with organizing gnosis, insights, and initiatory experience in the context of the magician's present incarnation.

The Web eventually gets so big that the spider cannot span its entirety with her eight limbs, so the mystic must delineate appointed times devoted to the several threads spun therein. Such times will be given by the spiritual power presiding over any given "cell," or else the magician must be alert to certain hours, days, months or cycles when their presence is most prominent.

Each "cluster" will have its own signs, spells and rituals. They embody the role they play in the magician's present incarnation and, through other links, their origin in some past life.

Therefore, all elements are bound in their exact alignments through intimate knowledge of both their karmic origin and subsequent evolution in the Thread or Chain of Being across Time! (Spoken by She-Who-Hath-No-Name)

She also says, *One must observe the dance of the Beloved - careful attention given to the greater and lesser cycles of the stars circling this brief but beautiful life.*

3.
The Nameless Substratum

The primordial substance is truly nameless in the sense that, despite its pervasive singularity, it cannot be attributed to any one principle worthy of name. Rather, it can only be known through its *temporal offspring*, distinct forms motivated by instincts, emotions, and insights considered "universal," yet always differing in terms of context. For instance, love never assumes the same nature, never generates the same conflicts, and seldom achieves a perfect resolution.

A spider web shares the same fate, if we establish an allegory upon purely physical observation.

Obviously a web is spun across "empty" space, supporting itself by clinging to stronger materials. As such, empty space, so called because air is invisible to the five senses, is ultimately necessary to 1) delineate unbound objects and 2) *to will the existence of the web*, through the agency of the spider's hunger for *flying prey*.

However, the causal function of this "empty space" isn't known until the web is perceived. Furthermore, our understanding of "web formation" arises from empty space, upon whose void nature each strand asserts its individuality.

Our sensory organs differentiate a spider's web from a knit blanket, coat, or tablecloth based on variation of "invisible presence" throughout. Physically, a web is not a tablecloth, and none of them are *the space*, yet this unacknowledged presence is the sole factor in differentiation!

To embody the Spider's power, one must *real-ize* this one truth:

That which you are not defines you!

Absence establishes another reality which always exists somewhere, defining our ambition (and by extension, our very selfhood) by its magnetic pull. We are all that we strive to achieve, be it This or That. The immortal beloved is both the shining light of truth, and the object of desire in whose Shadow we perpetually dwell, in the heat of earthly conflict. Our Goddess grants Insight to those who remember beauty, and instills Desire for none other than that which is timeless and true.

Thus Presence asserts itself in temporary absence, and continues to do so until all willing devotees are led to Her Kingdom.

In this sense we may reinterpret a passage from *Liber AL vel Legis* (Aleister Crowley's "holy book" of the New Aeon), when the space-marks are given their due presence:

There - is That, which Remains.

For now Her Beauty is *there*, beyond this earth, until She makes herself known through the remaining iconography of her noble nature, in the timeless artworks She inspired throughout the history of Mankind.

As such, the Space between us is the means to our ascent - departure from mortality, suffering, and strife through the mystery of Longing. Those that have departed always enchant in the perpetual mystery of Becoming.

As she tells me:

Invest Thyself!
Empty yourself into Another and you shall Be that which you are not-always.

Perhaps existence is to be upheld as an endless Be-longing, without *whom* nothing comes to pass. Indeed, the blood of the Dragon must be constantly stirred, heated, and forced to move across the channels of the earth, intoxicating and inspiring all to strive towards the pinnacle of Draconian consciousness.

4.
Silk and Salt of Space

Norse mythology gathers itself around a general consensus that the realm of Nifelheim contains eleven rivers flowing from a single source. This central well is known as Hvergelmir, from whose poisoned water emerge the rivers collectively known as *Elivagar*.

Nifelheim is one of the two worlds that emerged from the primordial void or "space" known as Ginnungagap. The other, called Muspelheim, is the necessary counterpart required in all acts of creation. In this case, Muspelheim and Nifelheim as Fire and Ice conceive all subsequent life forms through the dual process of melting and freezing. Heat melts unchanging realities into dynamic forms, these flowing outward and solidifying (i.e. cooling) once again into semi-permanent realities, establishing their presence as distinct variations of a single creative source (i.e. the act of procreation itself).

Such is the case with the Elivagar described as frozen waters of a rather salty and sulfuric nature, representative of the particular "poison" the magician encounters at various stages of Qliphothic initiation. In fact, all gnosis thereupon can be compared to a poison due to its sudden effect, whether this is intoxication, ecstasy, or painful medicine administered by the deities to awaken our latent psychic abilities.

The Draconian current, whose energy is akin to spontaneous combustion, is truly poisonous in this sense: we invoke immortal beings, whose existence lies beyond ourselves, to provide us with a remedy to human limitations in the form of power or knowledge. Since this power is also external, it is like a foreign substance to which our bodies must adapt. Some elements of "humanity" are necessarily destroyed, in order for the venom to reshape our body-soul complex in the likeness of the gods we summon.

For now, three such poisons are identified, corresponding to the paths guarded by Lucifer, Lilith and the Spider Queen. The first path administers the corrosive remedy to dogmatic ideology and strict logic (i.e. mathematics, philosophy, materialistic worldview), while the second excites the erotic aspect to seek only the most beautiful forms. As such they form a twin-process whose tension is resolved by the third elixir - Cohesion.

Through the third path, all conflict between intellect and instinct is brought to a standstill, bound into coherent compromise among the spider's silky threads. Truly, the nature of the Spider's venom is to numb tension, and to stabilize new insights emerging from initiatory exploration. Like the rivers freezing as they flow away from the primordial fire, the offspring of magical activity assume independent existence the further they stand from the center of the magician's web.

In this sense, we shall reformulate the Elivagar as silk, the substance required to spin the web across space. Like silk, they are fluid at first, eventually resting in stable form. The well of Hvergelmir is the dancing couple, the adept and immortal beloved who, like the primordial couple in Eden, proceed to name all things roaming the earth (i.e. the children they conceive, who remain somewhere along the threads, shining like constellations in space, bound only by the principle of correspondence previously written in silk and differentiated only by a nameless and omnipresent void).

The nature of the Elivagar, aside from its elemental composition, isn't described in Norse myth. The reader should take the names of each river as incantations to inspire personal exploration. Eventually, a unique iconography of sigils and spirits will weave themselves, giving the adept a unique symbolism serving as the mythical foundations of their own cosmic narrative. As such, we have here in the eleven rivers a new Tree of Qliphoth, whose details are at the discretion of the immortal beloved.

Their names are now given:

Svol, Gunnthra, Fjorm, Fimbulthul, Slidr and Hrid, Sylgr and Ylgr, Vid, Leiptr, Gjoll.

The reference to Norse paganism, in this case, reveals the necessity of specific examples in the dissemination of spiritual mechanisms. Indeed, all gods and goddesses are particular variations on a handful of archetypal themes found in the symphony of creation. Thus, every culture honors a unique embodiment for fertility, death, magic, love, and wisdom, while such forces are timeless and beyond all *names* spawned from an unknowable energy. Unknowable that is, unless *loved in the form she chooses at any given time, in the sweet perfume she distills to enchant our senses and excite our minds in the Imagining of new worlds.*

Thus shall the Spider Queen remain forever unknown, although several have linked her to ancient Greece or Egypt. Perhaps the closest approximation to her true essence is observed in designating her as some forgotten queen of Atlantis (whose existence is disputed by "pure science," but accepted by mystics who are no longer restrained by insistence on "physical proof").

Even better are those who *realize a new name* for her, unveiling another universe wherein she reigns. Honored by legions of eldritch giants, elder gods, and extra-terrestrial emissaries, the Nameless One still shines in some other face, another name echoing across empty space, among the silk threads spanning the circles of time.

Crawling All Over Me
Meditation and Ritual

Keona Kai'Nathera

For many nights, years ago, I have always had the same dream. I would be with my lover and while making love he would pin my arms down and vomit in my mouth. The vomit was of different species of snakes and spiders and other crawly things. I would constantly fight but to no avail. I could feel them pushing their way down my throat. I would wake up gagging, slapping at my face and hyperventilating.

What did that weird dream mean? Why was I having this disturbing dream almost every night for weeks? Whenever I was conscious and moving around, I would always see spiders, daddy long legs, very small species of spiders, medium size ones, and I would always be afraid.

Then in 2011 when I was interning at a government facility, I was bitten by a brown recluse spider. That was the consensus that the doctor told me when I went to the ER 5 days after being bit. I was waiting for the bus to go to the train station, and my building was on farmland acquired by the government on a main road. I never felt the bite, I never saw the spider, so it took time for me to feel something. He asked me how did I not see and feel a spider bite me? I said I have no clue. I only went to the ER because my foot was swelling, and I didn't notice it was starting to turn purple until I was back in the ER room. I had no issues with the antibiotics and no ill side effects.

Then around 8 years or so later, I was in contact with a young woman overseas who shipped me a bottle of dried tarantula and the fangs. Had no clue why I wanted it, but I did. As of now I still have both items. Just waiting for a reason to use it.

I found the Temple a few years later around 2013 or so and joined later, and I was taken aback and yet drawn to Arachne the first time I was in contact with her. I felt that with my experience I have a different attitude towards spiders. I normally freak out and spray them, like most people do. But I try my hardest to make sure that they are safe and unharmed. Last Samhain by brother gifted me with a spider ring, and I knew that it was about time to delve into the Spider Goddess and see what she must show me.

Meditation Supplies

These are the ingredients for the meditation:

- Dried tarantula
- Tarantula fangs
- White chime or tea candles (7) or a votive candle
- Salvia Divinorum (a hallucinogen tincture my friend sent me a while ago, but any hallucinogen will do, enough for 7 days)
- Black glass beaded spider
- Temple Sigil of Arachne (Page 36)

Meditation Prep

Set the fangs into the hallucinogen, and let it soak overnight. Roll the candles in hallucinogen and the dried spider. Let it dry overnight. Do this for all the candles. If using a tea light candle, sprinkle the dried tarantula on the candles after adding a few drops of the hallucinogen.

Meditation

Take 8 deep breaths. In for 4, hold for 4, out for 4. Vibe "*VOVIN*" or your own Enn for Arachne, while looking at her sigil. Let your mind relax and slide out onto the Draconian current. Once you are connected let the meditation begin.

Walking down a dark path you pass by various sizes of spiderwebs. Some of them have items in them, others have creatures you cannot place. Curiosity gets the best of you, and you wander closer to a web. It is beautiful. Shinning silver in the moonlight, reflecting small beads of round metallic crystals. There is a red velvet box in the middle of the web, wrapped with a black ribbon. You pluck the box out of the web and open it. Inside is a black glass beaded spider. It glows, with a hum emanating from it. You pick it up and place it in your left palm. As soon as it touches your warm hand, it wraps all 8 legs around your hand and plunges its fangs into your palm.

(AT THIS TIME PICK UP THE FANGS THAT HAVE BEEN INFUSED WITH THE HAALUCINOGEN AND PRESS THEM INTO YOUR LEFT PALM. IT IS YOUR PHYSICAL CONNECTION TO HER).

You immediately drop your left hand to your side, and she scatters back to her web. Your vison goes in and out, you fall to the ground, eyes still staring at the spider that is now morphing into the goddess herself. As your eyes are closing, she gets up and walks towards you. She whispers something in your ear... and you wake up on a path. Let the vision guide you.

You wake up with a throbbing of the head, dry mouth and a numb hand. It is dark now.

(AT THIS TIME LIGHT THE TEALIGHT CANDLE).

While the candle is burning to life, focus on the figure of Arachne fading into the distance. Sit with the candle for a few minutes and reflect on this connection to Arachne and where the vision took you.

Six Day Connection to Arachne

*It is recommended to do the 6 days to get the full message and absorb it, but you can also take one day to do all 6 items.

*Begin the meditation by vibrating *"VOVIN"* or your own personal Enn.

*Light a new candle for every day. Sit down comfortably or lay down but try not to fall asleep.

(Take some of your hallucinogen at this point to aid in your vision).

The light is illuminating you. In front of you she is sitting there. Her throne is red, her dress is black. Two of her arms are resting on the arm rests of her throne. The other six are holding various items for your journey. You will take each item, meditate on it and place it inside you.

Day 1 - Item 1: Hematite stone (transformation of negativity in your life).

Day 2 - Item 2: Spider Web (learning from past mistakes and moving forward).
Day 3 - Item 3: A Black Apple (knowledge of the path).
Day 4 - Item 4: Silver Chalice with black liquid (emotional balance).
Day 5 - Item 5: High Priestess Tarot Card (guide, communication and opening the mind).
Day 6 - Item 6: Black Water (rebirth).

Once you are finished with your vision, bring your attention back to Arachne and thank her. She has a bit of wisdom for you. After you are finished, stand up, turn around and walk back down the now moonlit path. Slowly come back to conscious and let your candle burn if it isn't already out.

Journal your experience daily.

You can bury the fangs on your property, or you can keep them on your altar to aid in communication and visions to Arachne.

Cobweb Meditation

Keona Kai'Nathera

In a dark room sit down in the lotus position or use a chair.

Otherwise, let your eyes adjust to the darkness around you. Feel the hum around you, feel the air cracking and slowly getting louder.

Your eyes are adjusted to the dark, and within the dark you see movement. You see small darker objects to your left, and then to your right. You see them hastening towards you and then stop. The objects move in front of you and slowly come towards you.

Minutes go by before you feel the first touch. Like feathers walking over your legs and up your thighs and soon up your arms. You want to flinch, to wipe them off, but you find you can't do anything but breathe fast. Then you hear:

"Relax."

So, you do. Ever so slightly you relax your muscles and let the sensation overtake you. By now your vision is flooded by a movement of blackness. They rush at you and crawl all over you at once. Your eyes are open, watching them start to spin their webs. They are wrapping you from all angles. The sensation is weird, tickling in some places, feathery in others.

The webbing is getting tighter and thicker. Then the movement stops. You feel a hum and slight vibration underneath you. It feels like something is opening and you drop.

Falling slowly through the darkness, you see a silver spider falling towards you. It gets larger as it approaches you and is slowly morphing into Arachne. You see her eyes, her smile, her hands reach for you.

She pulls you to her and you both slam into the ground. Your breath is knocked out of you. You inhale a black mist, turning you into a spider. Your eyes turn yellow, your body jerks and you turn over and run.

Where do you go? The cave to the left... The cave to the right... The cave in center.

You pick your choice and make a run from it. What awaits you inside is...

Let the vision take over. Write it all in your journal when you are released from the vision.

Dreamwork with Arachne

Keona Kai'Nathera

Cleanse yourself prior to going to bed. Have a glass of room temperature water. Sit down and vibrate VOVIN eleven times to align yourself with the Temple energy. Once you feel the hum and the connection to the Temple get up and lay down in bed. If you want to take a hallucinogen to aid in your vision, you may do so.

Once in bed, say this mantra: *"Arachne guide me down the web."*

As you are drifting to sleep, envision a path that is lined with silver webbing. As you are walking along the path, you see spiders following you. A few spiders step unto your path and walk in front of you. You notice the smells of the earth, the richness of the dirt. You see the dew sparkling off the leaves of the belladonna flower. Everywhere you walk you see spiders making intricate designs within their webs. Looking back in front of you, you see the spiders are ahead and standing in front of a dark cave with red lines running through it. As you move closer, the lines start to pulsate and hum. You continue walking and pick up the chalice on the left side of the opening. As you enter the cave, you pause, drain the cup and proceed down the path.

Continue the mantra from above or create your own. Let the vision unfold and write it down when you wake up. If you happen to wake in the middle of the night, repeat the mantra, take a few deep breaths and lay back down.

The Sigil of the Spider Goddess

Spider Goddess of the Qliphoth

Asenath Mason

This series of workings is centered on Arachne, the Spider Goddess of the Qliphoth, her Ophidian Current and her role in the self-initiatory magic of the Void. Originally, it was designed and conducted as one of the open projects held by the Temple of Ascending Flame. The workings have to be done on 6 days in a row, at any hour of the evening/night. They are designed to attune your consciousness to the Spider Current of the Void by assuming the god-form of Arachne - the weaver of the web that connects all manifestations of the Void, bridging the Tree of Life and the Tree of Death, darkness and light, the conscious and the unconscious. The first working opens the gateways for the energies of the goddess to enter your consciousness, allowing you to assume the spider form and place yourself in the center of the web. The following four days are dedicated to self-reflection and analysis of your personal path through meditation on the Four Magical Axioms, also known as the Four Powers of the Sphinx, and their shadow counterparts. The last ritual combines the work of the previous days into a powerful invocation of the Spider Current. The purpose of the project is to introduce the practitioner to the gnosis of Arachne, the Spider Goddess of the Void, through the concepts of Ophidian Venom and Spider Consciousness that are used in this work as self-initiatory tools within the magic of the Left Hand Path.

About Arachne

The name "Arachne" is derived from Greek mythology. According to the famous legend, she was a mortal woman, a weaver proud of her skills, who angered the goddess Athena by challenging her to a weaving contest and was cursed by the goddess to weave for all time. Since that moment Arachne's name has become ascribed to spiders (*Arachnida*), and all spider-like creatures are believed to be her children. The myth, however, has a much greater significance from the esoteric perspective. Her magical image is derived from the Ophidian cults and the Draconian/Typhonian tradition as described, for example, by Kenneth Grant in his *Typhonian Trilogies*. In this tradition, she is a primal Qliphothic goddess, the Queen of Space and the Weaver of the Web in the Void. The Web of Arachne should not be mistaken for a normal spider's web structured upon a plane surface. Extending across the Void, it has an intricate symmetry that links all existing planes and dimensions with infinitely tenuous threads of light, manifesting to a Nightside traveler as a network of tunnels and vortices. It bridges the gulf between the Dayside and the Nightside, waking and dreaming, the conscious and the unconscious.

The power of the Spider Goddess is the magical venom that is deadly to mundane consciousness but essential in the formula of initiation as it triggers the process of transformation through the inner alchemy of the mind. Just as a spider weaves the web, so we all weave our lives, making choices and shaping the structures of our universe. Through successive injection and absorption of particular venoms, the black kalas of the Goddess, the Initiate learns that all matter is illusion and it can be poisoned, dissolved, molded, shaped, etc. - decomposed and created anew. The world we live in is interconnected on various levels that work and interact with one another, thus weaving the web that forms the veil of illusion. What we perceive as "reality" is the outer picture of the whole process at a particular moment. We are in the center of this network, like a spider weaving and spreading its web across empty space. We pull strings, create new threads, link particular points in the network, etc., but it all happens in a random, uncontrolled way, as we can only see the outer picture. The structure behind it is hidden from our perception. Arachne teaches us that the root of all things is in the Void. Her venom dissolves mundane consciousness and opens the way to clear seeing. She shows us how to gaze through the veil of illusion and see the web itself, how to change and manipulate it at its roots, and by invoking her essence and absorbing her venomous kalas, we acquire the power to weave the web, thus becoming the true center of the universe and the very root of all manifestation.

Arachne usually manifests in a human form, as a beautiful woman with reptilian features or half-woman half-spider. Her hair is often made of snakes and she resembles the legendary Medusa, although Arachne's snakes are ghastly and woven from the substance of shadow. Sometimes she also comes in the form of a ghastly spider, black and monstrous. She bites the practitioner on the forehead to open and activate the Third Eye and injects venom into the aura to induce the astral transformation into a spider. The spider itself offers many interpretations, being an ancient symbol of growth and destruction, mystery and fate, poison and healing. In the Hindu lore, it represents Māyā, Illusion. At the same time, it stands for the understanding of our life choices, the art of manipulation of our destinies and the ability to maintain balance - between past and future, spiritual and physical, creation and destruction. Our choices and decisions are threads in the web, and like the spider's web they can either serve us or enslave us. The spider stands for the lesson that everything we do and experience now is weaving what we will encounter in the future, thus making us aware of our choices and allowing to take the reins of destiny into our hands. It is a perfect symbol for self-reflection, revaluation of our present lives and setting up long-term goals. This quality of the Spider Current will be used in the workings of this project in reference to the individual path of each practitioner.

The spider also typifies the female and feminine energy. The Spider Current embraces the magical kalas (essences) of the Lunar Goddess that are both dissolving and binding, venomous and healing, creative and annihilating. The Spider Goddess resides in the center of the Void, and while assuming her god-form we too become a focal point of our own world, gaining the ability to look at things from the perspective of the center. The creative and destructive powers of the Lunar Goddess are associated both with the spider and the serpent, and both animals are also zoomorphic totems of Arachne, as well as the scorpion that typifies her predatory and venomous qualities. This predatory aspect is especially reflected in the nature of the female spider that eats the male before, during, or after copulation, which also emphasizes the sexual nature of Arachne's mysticism. She is the weaver of fates, spinning and cutting the threads of life - creator and death. And she is also the symbol of rejuvenation and new beginnings, as both the spider and the snake shed their skin in order to grow. This ambivalence is characteristic of feminine currents and the spider is sometimes believed to symbolize the womb of the Mother Goddess that is both life-giving - spinning the web out of its own body, and deadly - aggressive and ensnaring. The Spider Goddess continuously builds and destroys her web, representing the ceaseless balance in the universe, but the center of the web is the devouring vortex that swallows everything. On the personal level, this symbolism is reflected in ceaseless alterations fundamental to the transformation of life - a sacrifice of the old for the building of the new.

The sigil used in the workings (Page 36) represents both the Spider Goddess and the Web of Fates. It includes the symbolism of the number eight, which signifies the eight legs of the spider, the number of the spider's eyes and the eight focal points in the work of the project. The central part of the sigil is symbolic of the lunar nature of the goddess and represents her womb out of which she spins her web. The feminine character of her current is emphasized by the image of the moon in the four phases of the lunar cycle. The skull represents the aggressive and deadly aspects of the spider, and the snakes are symbolic of her venom that is both the potion of immortality and lethal poison. The thorns in the outer points of the web signify the number eight as manifested through the polarity of four, in this work symbolizing the Four Magical Axioms, or the Four Powers of the Sphinx.

The Four Magical Axioms

The Four Powers of the Sphinx are derived from *Transcendental Magic* by the 19th-century French occultist Eliphas Lévi. They are: "To Know," "To Will," "To Dare," and "To Keep Silent." According to Lévi, these are indispensable conditions that a student of occult arts must include in their study. This view was highly influential in various magical philosophies in the previous centuries and incorporated in many occult systems. The Sphinx itself is a mystical and composite symbol - it has the head of a man, the torso and front legs of a lion, the rear end of a bull, and the wings of an eagle. These four creatures, combined into one, represent the union of elements and are associated with the symbolism of the number four. This symbolism includes the four cardinal directions, the four seasons, the four ages of man, and many others. Within the Sphinx all these elements are balanced, representing the image of the perfected man to which the student of occult arts should aspire, as they constitute the foundations and four pillars of the individual's ascent. On the other hand, the Draconian Initiate perceives the universe in all its aspects, including both the light and the shadow side of all things. Therefore, each magical axiom, or power, is also viewed from its negative perspective, thus constituting eight pillars on the Wheel of Fortune instead of four. This view is also discussed in *Time, Fate and Spider Magic* by Orryelle Defenestrate-Bascule, where the author speaks of four negative powers that are equally vital to attaining balance as the four magical axioms. These negative powers are: "To Know Not," "To Will Not," "To Dare Not," and "To Speak." Their meaning and value on the Path of the Dragon will be contemplated through the workings of this project through the "spider" perspective.

Why the spider? First of all, it corresponds to the number eight, embracing both the light and the shadow perspective of the four pillars of ascent, allowing us to see our personal path from multiple angles. The number eight is also a symbol of infinity, indicating cycles, evolution and passage of time - concepts associated with the spider symbolism and the mysticism of life and fate. The negative symbolism of the spider connects this zoomorphic totem with the Shadow Self and dark aspects of personality, life, magical path, etc., making the Spider Goddess of the Qliphoth a perfect god-form for the study and practice of their meaning and value. By assuming the god-form of Arachne we dissolve our personal universe and create a void in which we can view ourselves through the multiple eyes of the spider, from the perspective of non-attachment, seeing various components of our lives as particular points in the web that can be dissected, understood, manipulated, and rearranged to suit our personal goals. Just as a spider weaves its web across empty space, the consciousness of Arachne allows for bridging and integration of all parts and aspects of the Self into a whole, making the web a powerful vehicle of personal ascent.

The purpose of this work is to project this force into the Void and experience inner emptiness. In order to open yourself for the Current of Arachne, you will have to create a void in your consciousness and empty your mind so it may be filled by the consciousness of the Spider Goddess. This work may be a little frightening at first and if you do not feel comfortable with any of the workings provided in this project, do not perform them. If you choose to go on with all of them, it is recommended to perform your favorite Dragon/Kundalini meditation after each practice to balance your inner energies.

As you perform the workings, pay attention to all that happens around you during and after the rituals. Spiders and spider symbolism are often observed as being present all the time around the practitioner, manifesting as spiders appearing in various places, people unexpectedly talking about spiders, being bitten by spiders or other arachnids, or simply seeing things related to spiders in your day-to-day life. These manifestations of the Spider Current are also present in dreams, which are usually vivid and realistic, showing various situations, people and things important to you in various ways and from many different perspectives. Sometimes they are chaotic and random, bringing forth past and present issues. Other times they are magical and insightful, providing answers to questions asked during the meditations or simply enhancing the whole experience. However this current manifests to you, stay open to its influence both during the particular days of the project and in the days, or even weeks, following the workings.

Before the Rituals

Prepare your ritual space in the way you feel is suitable for this work. Place the sigil of the Spider Goddess on the altar. The sigil is provided on page 36 - you can print or draw it yourself and it has to be big enough to gaze into comfortably. If you wish to paint it, the recommended colors are black, silver and toxic green - a black sigil on a green background or silver on black will work best for this project. On your altar you may also put statues or images that represent the Spider Goddess or spider symbolism - these can be depictions of Arachne, diagrams of spider webs, or simply your personal seals or drawings that are somehow connected to this work. You may also choose to focus on the sigil alone, without any other decorations - this choice is entirely up to you. Apart from the sigil, you will need two candles - one red and one black. You may use more candles to light up the room, if you wish, but these two are perfectly enough for the whole project. You may also decorate your altar by placing offerings - flowers and poisonous plants representing the venomous nature of the goddess, a chalice filled with a liquid that has toxic qualities such as absinthe, obsidian skulls, spider jewelry, or other offerings reflecting the spider symbolism or associated with the Ophidian Current. Finally, you will need a wormwood oil to be used in the workings. If you cannot obtain it, feel free to replace it with another oil with similar bitter qualities.

It is recommended to perform the workings indoors, where you will not be disturbed, in complete silence and darkness. You will need the candles for certain parts of the workings but the meditations should be performed without any light and preferably without any sound. If you live in a city and complete silence is not really possible, you may use quiet dark ambient music in the background, such as Emme Ya, for example. You should also perform the workings alone - their purpose is to experience the solitude and emptiness of the Void. If you work with a partner, meditate together and separately, experimenting with both company and solitude in your practice.

Day 1
Opening the Gates to the Void

Light the black candle. If possible, this should be the only source of light in the room. Burn a strong incense - Dragon's Blood or the Nile Temple are the best for this work, but you may also use your favorite fragrance. Anoint your forehead with some wormwood oil, tracing the shape of an eye. Then sit in a comfortable position and put the sigil of the Spider Goddess in front of you. Do not look at the sigil yet. Instead, focus on the candle. See the flame and the darkness around it. Breathe deeply and each time you exhale, visualize your inner fire, warmth and light leaving your body and merging with the flame. At the same time, visualize that when you inhale, the darkness that surrounds you enters your lungs and spreads throughout the whole body, making it vibrate slightly. Continue this meditation until you become one with this dark essence, losing the sense of everything around.

Then anoint the sigil with your blood to open and activate the gateway to Arachne's current and focus all your attention on the image. See how the lines become charged and activated with your life substance. Visualize the sigil glowing and flashing with the toxic-green energy of the Spider Goddess. At the same time chant the mantra:

ARACHNIDIA-KA-RA-AN

Keep gazing at the sigil until you can easily memorize and visualize its shape. Then blow out the candle and close your eyes. Recall the image in your inner mind and see it crystallizing into the shape of the Spider Goddess. She is a beautiful woman, but her energy feels savage and predatory, as if she was only wearing a human skin. Her eyes are emerald, she has the forked tongue of a snake, and her hair is made of ghastly serpents, writhing and hissing. She is naked and snakes are coiling around her. Their venom drips on the ground and turns into smoke - poisonous, toxic and suffocating. It forms into other serpentine shapes and ghastly spiders that swarm around you. In her hands she is holding a chalice filled with venom. As you drink the essence of her current, you can feel yourself transforming and assuming the form of a spider. For a moment everything disappears and you are now alone in the black space, inside a huge spider web made of threads of silver light. Explore how it feels to be the spider in the center of the web, let the visions flow freely and open yourself for the experience. You may also ask the goddess to teach you how to move through the web and manipulate the particular threads.

When you feel it is time to end the meditation, open your eyes and light the red candle. Focus again on the flame, this time reversing the flow of energies - when you exhale, visualize the darkness leaving your body and the fiery energy entering your lungs when you breathe in. You may choose to skip this closing practice, leaving yourself opened for the energies of the Spider Current throughout the whole project, but if you feel unbalanced after the working, this simple exercise will help you get back in balance.

The body of the spider is full of new possibilities, new perspectives and insights, and also new powers to gain and develop. The threads in the web can be used to trigger visions of both yourself and other people at a certain point in their life, be it past, present or future. It can also be used to move across the Void and explore various realms of the Nightside, Qliphothic worlds, concepts such as Atlantis or Shamballah, or various parts of the underworld - both in the universal and individual meaning of the term. There are also thoughts of the spider as a force of creation, and you may be given a glimpse into what it is like to spin the web (manifest energy of creation) out of the womb, giving birth to manifestations of a magical intent. Being in the center of the web is also experienced as being connected to everything, providing a sense of deep unity with the entire personal universe. This feeling is sometimes dreamy and slightly energy-draining, as if the force was sucked into the Void. Other times it is experienced as chaotic and confusing, producing a series of visions flashing before the eyes and changing quickly without taking any concrete shape. Some practitioners find it easy and natural to transform into a spider, while others struggle with personal barriers and need more time to get used to the energies of the current. Therefore, if you do not succeed immediately, do not get discouraged - keep practicing until you get there.

Day 2
The First Power of the Sphinx

The purpose of this working is to invoke the Spider Current and assume the god-form of Arachne to meditate on the first magical axiom - "To Know," and its shadow counterpart – "To Know Not." This concept is associated with the element of air and mental faculties. It represents intellect, mentality and learning. It is the drive to pursue knowledge, contemplate the universe and our place in it, seek answers to our questions, and evolve through study and experience. It is also associated with seership and vision of things unknown, hidden, existing beyond the scope of mundane perception. The symbolism of this axiom includes the direction of east, youth and the formative years in the life of man, dawn, and spring in the earth's cycle. Its shadow counterpart, "To Know Not," is usually interpreted in a negative way, but on the other hand, it represents innocence found in the mind of a child that is yet about to explore the world. It is spontaneity and the bliss of discovery, knowledge not subjected to any form of conditioning. This interpretation is especially vital in the magic of the Qliphoth, where we continuously revaluate what we have learned, often facing the necessity to reject all that we know and learn to look at the universe from completely new angles and perspectives. This possibility appears when we assume the "spider" consciousness - and this is what we will explore in this and the other workings that follow.

Begin this practice in the same way as the day before: prepare the temple, light the black candle and burn some incense. Anoint your forehead with wormwood oil, tracing the shape of an eye. Focus on the breathing cycle combined with the candle flame meditation and fill yourself with the essence of darkness. When you are ready to continue, speak the words of invocation:

Arachne, Weaver of the Web,
Open the Gates to the Nightside and lead me into the
Womb of the Dragon.
Let me see the world with the Eyes of the Spider,
And show me what it means To Know and To Know Not!

Then move your focus to the sigil. Again, chant the mantra of calling: *ARACHNIDIA-KA-RA-AN* until you feel the energies of the Void flowing through the sigil into the room, connecting you with the goddess and her current. Visualize the sigil growing bigger and bigger, until it becomes a huge spider web around you, and at the same time envision yourself transforming into the spider. Then stop chanting, blow out the candle and continue the meditation in darkness and silence.

Visualize yourself as the spider in the center of the web. It has eight outer points, and at the end of each there is a pyramid. There are four bright pyramids shining with silver light and four black pyramids absorbing all light. The bright pyramids represent the four magical axioms in their positive meaning, the black ones - their shadow counterparts. These pyramids stand for the pillars/foundations of your magical path. The purpose of the meditation is to identify them, explore their meaning and understand how they influence your life. Visualize the magical axiom "To Know" on the doors of one of the bright pyramids and "To Know Not" on one of the black ones. Then enter both and explore what this axiom means to you - how it empowers or weakens your personal development. Do not try to feel or live it - *see it* as if you were watching a movie in which you are the main character. Ask yourself questions - Do you put enough time and attention in the process of learning? Do you keep records of what you have learned so that your knowledge will not be lost? What prevents you from learning? What drives you to seek knowledge? What kind of knowledge makes you grow and what is redundant on your personal path? Visualize these questions taking shapes. Observe how they are interconnected and learn to understand these interactions and influence them. Take as much time as you need for this meditation.

When you feel ready to end the working, open your eyes and return to your mundane consciousness. If you wish, you may now light the red candle and meditate for a while on the inner fire, or you may simply close the working.

The four magical axioms are usually experienced as separate and dualistic, but also interconnected, seen as two parts of the same concept. Visually, they are observed on the pyramids in the form of writing or pictures, or as swirling vortices inside the pyramids. The first axiom is often seen in the form of an open eye, while its negative counterpart takes the shape of a closed eye - representing the knowledge and lack of it, awareness and ignorance, understanding and blindness. Sometimes the vision of the concept manifests as a library, warehouse, or simply a room full of bookshelves, trunks or various containers - places associated with knowledge and learning. They represent things forgotten, repressed and pushed down into the unconscious, as well as those that are yet to be learned. There are thoughts of fear to take these things out, confront them and make them conscious. There are also visions of people and places related to the personal life of the practitioner and their magical path - some of them empowering the spiritual journey, others standing as an obstacle to personal development - all connected by the threads in the web, thoughts of things that are already known and those that we are eager to learn. Knowledge is an important part of the magical process, as it is often essential to know the theory behind the practice, and the theory must be tested and validated, thus leading to "understanding." Otherwise, knowledge without understanding can make us arrogant and over-confident without justification. There are many observations about knowledge, understanding and experience being interconnected on many levels in this work, all of them essential in the initiatory process, according to the pattern: Knowledge-Understanding-Wisdom. Knowledge of magical rites, symbolism, spirits, deities, etc., provides foundations for spiritual development and can be used as tools of practical sorcery. Knowledge defeats ignorance, makes us strong and assertive in a lot of situations. On the other hand, lack of knowledge is the driving force that motivates to continue learning and growing. It is the unpredictability that makes life and magical initiation a constant mystery that can only be known through experience. Without preconceived notions, it is easier to develop clear-seeing, or clairvoyance, as the vision is not obstructed by imposed patterns of thinking. Knowledge without experience can be worthless, as it is not understood and validated, and thus, cannot be successfully applied. Magic without learning can lead to delusions, as we have no means to root ourselves and become balanced. But then again, the lack of knowledge can make us insecure and afraid to transcend our boundaries. Knowledge is also power over the universe - we can control things and people if we know enough about them and if we know how to use this knowledge to our advantage. From the Spider Current perspective, "To Know" is to create the thread in the web, to "Un-Know" is to absorb the thread back into the essence. The web contains both knowing and "un-knowing" - things that we are aware of and those that are yet to come. However, this is not a fixed pattern - by getting to the source we can change and shape it, thus each thread in the web may lead to a multitude of possibilities. It is knowledge that makes the creation and destruction of the web possible.

Day 3
The Second Power of the Sphinx

The second magical axiom is „To Will" and its shadow counterpart is "To Will Not." This concept corresponds to the element of fire and represents inspiration and passion. It is enthusiasm that prompts us to action, impulse to create, desire to act. It is the flame behind our intentions and pursuits - the driving force on the magical path. Symbolically, it is associated with the direction of south, adolescence and young adulthood, midday, and summer. Its dark counterpart represents inaction and passive existence in its negative meaning, but it may also be viewed as a mastery of passions and wisdom of how to rule our desires and not to be enslaved by them. Fire itself is ambivalent and its symbolism is interpreted in many ways. Passions can drive us to action and burn obstacles on our way, or they can consume us if we cannot control them. They can make us grow or they can be a tool of self-destruction. In Draconian magic, fire is used to purge our intentions, inspire our actions, and destroy that which prevents us from growing, often leaving the landscape of our world bare and black - the empty canvas of the Void on which we can rebuild our personal universe, like a spider spinning its web across empty space.

Like the day before, start the meditation with preparing the temple, light the black candle and burn some incense. Again, anoint your forehead, focus on the candle meditation and fill yourself with the essence of darkness. When you are ready to continue, speak the words of invocation:

Arachne, Seducer and Devourer,
Guide me through the Web of Desires into the Heart of the
Void.
Show me the world through the Eyes of the Spider,
And reveal to me what it means to Will and to Will Not!

Move your focus to the sigil and start chanting the mantra *ARACHNIDIA-KA-RA-AN*. Feel the energies of the Void flowing through the sigil into the room, connecting you with the goddess and her current. Envision that it grows and expands into the huge web around you, while you are the spider in the center of the Void. Take as much time as you need to build this image in your mind. Then stop chanting, blow out the candle and continue the meditation in darkness and silence.

Again, envision the eight pyramids at the outer points of the web. This time focus on the axiom "To Will," visualizing it on the doors of one of the bright pyramids, and "To Will Not" on one of the black ones. Then enter both and explore what this axiom means to you and how it empowers or weakens your personal development. Meditate on your passions and desires and ask yourself questions - Are you strong-willed? What inspires you on your path and what puts you off? Are you in control of your desires or do they control you? What drives you to action and magical practice? Do you use your inner fire to overcome obstacles on your path? Can you use it to fight laziness and fatigue? Are you a creative person? Visualize these questions taking shapes and observe how they are interconnected. Learn to understand these interactions, influence them and use them as tools of your personal growth. Let the experience flow freely and take as much time as you need for this meditation.

When you feel ready to end the working, open your eyes and return to your mundane consciousness. Light the red candle and meditate on the inner fire, or close the working at this point.

This axiom often manifests in various forms representing fire - for example, as two flames, one normal and the other inverted - symbolic of the negative meaning of the whole concept. The focus of this work is also on emotions, and there are many thoughts about the power of emotions and energy contained within them, observations about desire, strength of will or lack of it, self-discipline, actions, etc. Emotions should be directed and connected to the right actions and anticipated outcomes. "To Will" means to continuously acquire and maintain power to accomplish our goals, while "To Will Not" represents passive attitude, which, however, may not necessarily be something bad. It is about trusting our intuition, observing the world and applying the force of inertia left by other people for our own purpose. It can be an attitude of non-attachment, developing the ability to see ourselves from another perspective, and thus allowing to determine what empowers us and what stands as an obstacle to our personal ascent. Moments of stillness are important as they let our energies get back to balance - they make us focused and ready to plant the seeds of our will. This axiom corresponds to patience, which is characteristic for a spider that builds its web patiently, renewing it when it gets damaged or destroyed, and patiently waits for the prey to be caught in the threads. Desire can be a positive force when it motivates and drives us to action, but it can also distract us from what we already have, create obsessions and drain our life-force, making us feel as if we were trapped in a spider web, enveloped in a cocoon and slowly losing the vital energy. When we control the desire, we become truly free, no longer enslaved by our urges. We can really experience the Void then, and we can focus on the here and now instead of chasing empty dreams. On the other hand, desire and passion is what drives and fuels us toward our goals. Passion is an essential component of all magic as it is pure energy that can be raised, directed and used to manifest the intent. The Dragon Force/Kundalini manifests as emotions - if we suppress them, we lose energy. If we direct them, the energy works for us. Fire will always both warm and burn us, and neither of this can be avoided.

Day 4
The Third Power of the Sphinx

The third magical axiom is "To Dare" and its dark counterpart is "To Dare Not." It corresponds to the element of water and the realm of emotions, intuition and psychic faculties such as clairvoyance or clairaudience. It is the mystical and the elusive, dreams and visions, the mystery of what lies beyond the mundane senses. It is also the feminine, as water is the symbol of the Lunar Goddess - the womb, the concept of birth-death-rebirth, the ability to regenerate. Its symbolism is associated with the direction of west, older adulthood and the onset of being elderly, dusk/sunset, and autumn as a season. Magical practices that correspond to the element of water are those of intuition, scrying, divination, and connection with the Other Side. Magical powers associated with it are those of letting go and floating with the current, or the opposite - directing the energies of the current to manifest our will. Water can be still and calm, as well as fierce and roaring, ruthlessly taking all that stands in the way. This reflects the idea of "daring," which is also connected with courage, stepping out of our safety zone and confronting our Shadow Self - demons and monsters that lurk in depths of the unconscious. Lack of this audacity may prevent our progress on the path, but "To Dare Not" also means being cautious and taking our steps with consideration and responsibility. It is the wisdom of when to move and when to wait, using our intuition for self-judgment and taking advantage of the best opportunities offered to us by the universe.

Again, start the meditation with preparing the temple, light the black candle and burn incense. Anoint your forehead with wormwood oil. Focus on the candle meditation and fill yourself with the essence of darkness. When you are ready to continue, speak the words of invocation:

Arachne, Spinner of Fates,
Teach me how to weave the Web across the Ocean of
Time.
Let me gaze through the Eyes of the Spider,
And show me what it means to Dare and to Dare Not!

Move your focus to the sigil and start chanting the mantra *ARACHNIDIA-KA-RA-AN*. Feel the energies of the Void flowing through the sigil into the room, connecting you with the goddess and her current. Again, envision that it grows and expands into the huge web around you and visualize yourself as the spider in the center of the Void. Take as much time as you need to build this image in your mind. Then stop chanting, blow out the candle and continue the meditation in darkness and silence.

Visualize the eight pyramids at the outer points of the web and the axiom "To Dare" on the doors of one of the bright pyramids and "To Dare Not" on one of the black ones. Then enter both and explore what this axiom means to you and how it empowers or weakens your personal development. Recall situations in which you stood up to confront your personal issues and those when you stepped back from the fight. Did it make you feel strong or weak? What issues are still waiting to be faced? Are you ready to step out of your comfort zone and face the challenges of the path, even if they come with risk? Meditate on your psychic skills and ask yourself questions - Can you use your intuition as a magical tool? Can you gaze into the Other Side and communicate with its denizens? Visualize these questions taking shapes and observe how they are interconnected. Learn to understand these interactions, influence them and use them for your personal growth. Let the experience flow freely and take as much time as you need for this meditation.

When you feel ready to end the working, open your eyes and return to your mundane consciousness. Close the working or light the red candle and meditate for a moment on your inner fire.

In the context of this axiom, the spider web can be viewed either as a comfortable zone, creating the feeling of safety and protection, or a trap which prevents us from moving forward. This distinguishes the spider from the fly - the spider is in the center of the web, controlling it, defining its patterns, and waiting to move, while the insect flies into the web blindly and gets entangled. This is a metaphor of a magician who knows when to act and when to wait in order to attain one's goals as opposed to a person who acts in a random way, getting trapped in pursuits of illusory goals. On the one hand, not daring to act is a sign of weakness and may deepen our fears and personal inhibitions, making the obstacles pile up on the path instead of confronting and defeating them. On the other hand, we must always trust our intuition and move at the right moment and in the right direction. Random and chaotic actions may not get us where we want to be. While "To Dare" means to move forward and overcome our barriers, "To Dare Not" means to remain in one place - it is the lack of motion, but also the phase of rest after another action and gathering back the energy to continue. It is also a combination of knowledge and intuition and the time of assessing the chances of success. Both attitudes can trigger positive and negative phenomena - from fear, anxiety and paranoia to megalomania and ego-trips. In visions, this axiom sometimes manifests in the form of a door, which is open in its positive meaning and closed in its negative counterpart. The insights connected with this vision are about following the intuition, swimming with the current, being careful and attentive, but also about facing challenges on the path. It is essential to confront them, but sometimes we have to withhold and regroup, gather the forces and then deal with the situation. Courage is important but only if it goes together with responsibility, while senseless bravery rarely leads to victory. These meditations also come with a lot of emotions, reminding us about our failures, but also releasing anger and fury in a positive, motivating sense. When we fall, we need to get up and keep going, stronger and empowered by the experience. Many people choose to be victims and complain all the time about their misery, but they never do anything to change it. The fear of change often binds us and does not let us move forward. Daring in magic is difficult - it is about letting go and flowing with the current, having full faith that it will take us where we should be, as well as staying in control of the process and making conscious decisions - the key to understanding the power of this magical axiom is to keep balance between these two seemingly contradictory attitudes.

Day 5
The Fourth Power of the Sphinx

The fourth magical axiom is "To Keep Silent" and its negative counterpart is "To Speak." This concept is associated with the element of earth and the symbolism that represents the underworld, the unconscious, or the "buried," repressed parts of the Self. It signifies things solid, material, secure - those foundations of your magical path that are tangible and manifested in your mundane life. It also corresponds to the direction of north, elderly and old age, midnight, and winter. In magical practice, the power of earth is associated with patience, endurance, inner stillness, grounding, centering, shielding, and the ability to channel energies of other dimensions onto the physical plane. It is the power of manifestation that binds and integrates the other powers into a coherent whole. It is also wisdom and maturity on the path that allows us to recognize situations in which we should keep silent and those that require us to speak. In old magical traditions, boasting about success in magical operations was believed to draw jealous spirits, the evil eye, or other forms of malediction, be it from another magician or the world of spirits. Silence was a virtue also for many other reasons. On the other hand, speech is a power in itself - as a magical tool it can bless or curse. It is also the tool of the teacher who passes secrets of magic to a student. Sharing what we have learned on our path may help others who have not progressed that far yet. It is also a token of gratitude to the universe for revealing its mysteries to us up to this point. Word made flesh is a powerful manifestation of our personal will, knowledge and courage, an important pillar of our personal ascent.

Prepare the temple, light the black candle and burn incense. Anoint your forehead with wormwood oil and start the meditation by focusing on the candle flame to fill yourself with the essence of darkness. When you are ready to continue, speak the words of invocation:

Arachne, Black Womb of the Universe,
Guide me on the pathways of the Underworld of my Soul,
Let me gaze through illusions of the world with your
Spider eyes,
And show me what it means To Keep Silent and To Speak!

Again, move your focus to the sigil and start chanting the mantra *ARACHNIDIA-KA-RA-AN*. Feel the energies of the Void flowing through the sigil into the room, connecting you with the goddess and her current. Visualize that it grows and expands into the huge web around you and envision yourself as the spider in the center of the Void. Take as much time as you need to build this image in your mind. Then stop chanting, blow out the candle and continue the meditation in darkness and silence.

Visualize the eight pyramids at the outer points of the web and the axiom "To Keep Silent" on the doors of one of the bright pyramids and "To Speak" on one of the black ones. Then enter both and explore what this axiom means to you and how it empowers or weakens your personal development. Ask yourself questions - Can you use the power of speech to manifest your will? Are you grounded and balanced in your magical practice? When do you speak about your work and when do you keep silent? Can you earth what you have learned through this work? Are you patient in your practice? Visualize these questions taking shapes and observe how they are interconnected. Learn to understand these interactions, influence them and use them as tools of your personal growth. Let the experience flow freely and take as much time as you need for this meditation.

When you feel ready to end the working, open your eyes and return to your mundane consciousness. Light the red candle and meditate on the inner fire, or close the working.

In visions, this axiom sometimes manifests in the form of an open and closed mouth, inside of which is a vortex of darkness. Like the other axioms, it conveys an ambivalent meaning that can be understood in many positive and negative ways. Speech or voice itself carries energy, and like any form of energy, it can be channeled and directed into an intent. Words are energy and can be used to heal and bring comfort, as well as curse and evoke fear. We can manipulate others by the power of speech and gain control over them if we know how to do it successfully. Words can make people our friends or enemies - it is an extremely powerful tool that can do as much good as evil. In magic, the power of speech makes our will manifest and shapes the universe. It is essential to declare what we want to achieve to accomplish our goals. A word spoken in the proper place and time can truly alter destiny. It carries the power of creation, manifesting and spreading around us like a spider web. On the other hand, "To Speak" is also to waste energy - meaningless gossip, conversations that bring no learning, causal chit-chat - they all drain and weaken us. "To Keep Silent" is to remain focused on ourselves. It is the state of meditation that helps us hear our inner voice and communicate with the unconscious, giving insights into ourselves, as in silence we are not disturbed by outer factors. There is also the question of keeping silent about magic that is associated with the traditional meaning of the axiom. It is important to speak about our magical activity and results to people of similar interests - sharing the experience to validate our knowledge and learn new things from others or to contribute to the knowledge of others, while remaining silent in the company of those who would not understand what we do and why we do it. But then again, in the modern world with global means of communication that allow information to travel fast, it is not entirely possible to keep silent - we have to speak, but the key is to say only as much as needed and in the proper way. It is all about the correct use of words to manifest our will. Speaking is a way of exchanging energy, too. We can draw energy from others by stirring their emotions and reactions by speaking to them. We can also channel and focus energy from the other planes by certain words of power in a ritual. Other thoughts on this magical axiom may refer to various means of communication and manifestation - words are but one medium, but a person may also "speak" through art, music and other forms of self-expression - and this is one of the most important qualities in magic.

Day 6
The Rite of the Spider Goddess

Prepare your temple like on the previous days. This time you may also choose to include the sacrament - pour a strong alcohol with toxic/hallucinogenic qualities, possibly absinthe, into the chalice and put it on the altar to represent the venom of the Spider Goddess. The sacrament, however, is optional and not absolutely necessary in this ritual.

Anoint your forehead, light the black candle, and stand or sit in a comfortable position. Again, begin this practice with the candle meditation to absorb the energies of the Void, and then focus on the sigil and for a moment chant the words of calling: *ARACHNIDIA-KA-RA-AN.* Feel the energies flowing through the sigil and Arachne's presence in the temple, awaiting invitation to enter your consciousness and transform it into the spider. When you feel ready to perform the ritual, begin the invocation:

In the name of the Dragon,
Primal Source of All Creation,

I open the Gates to the Void to weave the Web of Infinity.
For I am Arachne, the Spider Goddess,
She who opens secret gateways between dimensions
And teaches the art of travelling through the pathways of
the Spider.
I am Arachnidia,
I am Ka-Ra-An,
She who rises to consume the world in her venom.
I am the goddess of a thousand names and a thousand
faces.
She who holds all gifts and powers of life and death,
Who weaves Chaos from Order and Order from Chaos.
I am the chalice of venom and divine nectar, the source of
wisdom and inspiration.
I am the Queen of the Dead and I bring death and rebirth
in the Womb of the Dragon.
I am the mother and the destroyer.
I am the black elixir of transformation, change and
becoming.
I am the black womb of the universe,
She who delivers all life and devours it when mortal flesh
crumbles into dust.
I am the Queen of the Night who wakes the dead and puts
the living to eternal sleep.
I am the mother of shadows.
I am the Seducer of Souls and the Devourer of Gods.
I am the spider that spins the web across all worlds and
dimensions.
I am the mistress of dreams and I guide the soul through
realms of nightmares and fantasies.
I am the Serpent, the Spider and the Moon.
Those who seek my knowledge I guide between spaces and
angles.
Those who do not dare to face me I trap in my web and
devour.
I am the mystery of life and death, light and darkness, day
and night.

*I spin my Web of Destiny and create my own path to
Infinity.
I am the Spinner, the Weaver and the Cutter.
I am Arachne!*

When you finish the words of invocation, blow out the candle
and sit or lie down. If you have chosen to include the
sacrament, let it absorb the energies of the ritual and drink
it, thus absorbing the essence of the Spider Current. Focus
again on the image of the web and envision yourself as the
spider in the center of the Void. Visualize the eight pyramids
as well, and all eight magical axioms. This time, however, take
a step further - visualize that the outer points of the web
move toward you from all around, merging into one pyramid
in the center. At first, envision yourself inside of it, then
visualize that the pyramid disappears, too, and you are alone
in the black space. For a moment everything disappears and
then you *become* the web yourself. Your aura shines with
silver light, shooting out countless silvery threads, forming
the web that extends in all directions, no longer limited to
eight, but expanding to hundreds or more. These threads
connect you to each single moment of your life - past,
present and future; each person and object that is a part of
it; every step on your path you have taken so far and are yet
to take. With your multiple spider eyes you can see how they
are interconnected, explore the "karmic lessons" behind
events and things happening in your life, and you can also
influence these events, taking the reins of destiny into your
hands. Ask yourself questions about your goals and choices
- How are they affecting your life? Are they improving your
personal development? How can you make your path more
effective, more inspiring, more powerful? Ask the goddess to
guide you through labyrinths of your soul and let her
manifest and speak to you through your inner mind, showing
you your personal powers and weaknesses. Open yourself for
the experience and let it flow freely.

When you wish to end the meditation, open your eyes and light the red candle. Focus again on the flame and fill yourself back with the Dragon's Fire. This meditation is not optional this time - it is strongly recommended to use it as the final practice of the project. Take a look at your visions and experiences from the whole project and meditate on what you have learned through this work and how it may affect your future steps on the path. Let this final day be the time of reflections and perhaps new inspirations in your personal work.

The purpose of this working is closure and focusing the energies of the Spider Current. This comes with reflections on the meaning of the four (eight) axioms and their combined powers. There are also powerful manifestations of the Spider Goddess. Sometimes it is a very potent working, opening the way to the Current of Arachne. Other times it is calm and quiet, not producing any strong effects but bringing the energies to balance. The practice of becoming the web itself brings the feeling of being connected to everything and being able to access the power from all directions in time and space. There are thoughts of the inner world and the outside world and how they are interconnected through the web, bridging the conscious and the unconscious. You may experience many visions and thoughts passing through your mind like a kaleidoscope of images, changing fast, often random and seemingly unconnected, but forming a greater picture if seen at their roots. This is accompanied by thoughts of how everything is connected and affected by one another. There are also observations on the connection between past and future and how our past actions affect the present, and how the present actions will affect the future. The spider consciousness allows to see these connections and change them, cutting, weaving, and shaping our destiny - showing us how to destroy the web and free ourselves from that which binds us, as well as how to change ourselves through the spider venom that poisons consciousness and shifts our perceptions. The venom of the spider is both powerful and deadly, a potent tool to change consciousness and a dangerous weapon against the ego and that which we see as a threat to ourselves. It is a raw energy of the Void that can be channeled and applied for practical use.

This is the day of self-reflection and recognizing your strengths and weaknesses, thinking of what to empower and what to leave behind on the path - what to focus on and what obstacles need to be removed from your way in order to improve your personal development and to become the Spider - the true Weaver of Fate.

The Cocoon of Arachne & The Gift of Poison

Charlie Demos

Items needed for the ritual:

The Sigil of Arachne drawn by your own hand on black or purple paper with silver pen/marker:

- 1-3 black candles
- a blood-letting tool

Arrange your candles around the sigil with one in the center and the other two on the left and right sides respectively. Speak these words as you are preparing them.

The middle pillar candle: **CONNECTION**
The left: **RESPECT**
The right: **INTENTION**

Meditate briefly on these statements of affirmation.

BREATH WORK:
Raising the Dragon Fire

With eyes closed, turn your gaze up to the third eye and begin the dynamic, rapid and sharp inhaling and exhaling (*Kapalabati breathing*) while speaking in your mind *"VOVIN."* Do this for 3-9 minutes.

Mark the sigil with drops of blood on the innermost circular point first. Then anoint further on all outer arrow points that lead back into the center.

Qliphothic Breathing:

Begin *Qliphothic or shadow* breathing for 7-11 minutes with each cycle envisioning an expansion of your will, a swelling of your psychic field. Imagine sucking back into yourself all the energy you have produced, accordion fanning the brilliant flames of the Dragon, fueling ascension first like a hot air balloon gently floating into a jarring shapeshifting rocket. See the moment of your soul bursting out of your crown to hover above your body. This is intentionally instantaneous. With extreme attention to detail, document all sensations and any feelings of needing to hold on to this moment.

Unwinding the Hands of Time, Drawing Down the Crown of Arachne Saturnine

The crown of Arachne contains an infinite multiplicity of eyes that can reveal unique vantage points otherwise imperceptible to the magician. Arachne can illuminate the most shrouded of blind spots, exposing the darkest corners of our subconscious while allowing for a reconstruction of psychic architecture. Wickedly powerful webbing to not only create our own reality but also to facilitate movement from stagnancy and blindness to evolution and clarity.

While continuing Qliphothic breathing, visualize a clock. This can be whatever is aesthetically pleasing to you. Begin to focus on the number 11. With each breath cycle, visualize the number dissolving. What shape does each number take? Do they crumble, explode, unfold, transform, disappear? Document *every* detail for yourself through this process. Once you have worked counterclockwise from 11-1, you will reach 12. Notice how the number 12 easily interlocks to one shape: the sigil of Saturn. Charge that shape with your Draconian consciousness, visualize your God/Goddess flame pouring out from your third eye into the shape as it begins to catch fire. Form your crown from breath, heat, visualization. Infuse it with the most supreme expression of your creative aesthetic. The rebirth of regality in levitation. Draw the crown of Arachne onto your head and feel the lugubrious Saturnine mysteries flooding your consciousness. You are now prepared to work outside the brutal prison of "time" as you have temporarily destroyed the construct of human limitation. Abject darkness. Introverted heavy sensual immersion. No restrictions. This is the genesis point to construct and explore the pathworking.

Pathworking: The Cocoon of Arachne

Visualize dynamic gold and red flames that begin to spark and emerge from your blank landscape. The bold, dramatic, ostentatious inferno alchemizing into slick black flame. Moving through an obsidian pyramid 10 inches above your head, your soul begins to ascend from your temple into the infinite darkness of space. The cosmic landscape twinkles and vibrates with a universal power. Begin to notice how the silver light of the stars and moon start to liquify and spin dynamically, forming a beautiful thread. A giant shadow figure begins to form in your line of sight. It is Arachne as she emerges out of the expansiveness of space, pulling planets and galaxies to form her body. Face her with respect and honor, begin the invocation.

The Invocation of Arachne:

I invoke you, Goddess Arachne
Queen of space and the cosmos
Spider woman of the void
Empower my ritual
Spin your cosmic cocoon around me
Sequester me, contain me in your grand design
Fill my veins and breath with your poison
So I may reclaim my life force,
my power from all connections both near and far.
Allow me to stretch my consciousness far and beyond the
edges of reality to steal back what has always been mine.
I revoke all bonds and ties.
To the pithy, weak, and wicked ones who have sought my
demise,
To those who seek to drain my life force, feed on me and
keep me tied to their toxicity
May they receive a gift of poison.
May they experience me as noxious deadly paralysis!

Brilliant Goddess Arachne, divine seamstress of universal creation.
fill my heka with your Venom, propel forth my will and intention.

Continue with the regular breathing or the Qliphothic technique (I prefer the latter), visualizing Arachne spinning her web. Thick, sticky ropes of her cosmic fluid web form a solid cocoon around you. Feel the energy of gestation; momentary stasis. Claim for yourself this sacred space in where you will become the next form of your necessary evolution.

When you feel it's time: Rip open, out and up, ascending anew, burning with light and poison. Notice the form you have taken and begin to feel the sensory aspects of transformation.

Then begins the verbal mantra:

"NEXUM DISSOLUTO"

Speak this incantation with conviction and authority 13 times with the movement prescribed below.

With your arms form an "X" over your chest for NEXUM and dynamically uncross them to straight arms suspending in tight muscular contraction horizontally on either side of you for "DISSOLUTO."

Imagine every thread of light, every tie being unknotted and pulled back to you. It's like watching something in reverse, pulling back your essence that lingers in places they do not belong. Then visualize green waves of poison flowing from your veins. It's a maelstrom of fire and ice; acidic, noxious, lethal. Allow this poison to settle into place, filling the space of that which has been returned to its source.

When you feel it's time, ground yourself back into mundane consciousness and record your findings.

Øliphothic Ritual Reflections with Arachne as Initiatrix, Muse and Guide

Charlie Demos

1.
The Inevitability of Rawness

Wide open space. Wild naked musings.
Spread eagle spitting spurts of saliva lubrication fuel for expulsion of demented boundaries.
GET BENT.
Soft subtle flirtatious scent of gardenia, heliotrope, orange flower. I become tipsy.
Dull white haze of warm wet softness dripping slowly, willingly diminutive against monstrous silence... The inevitability of rawness.

Ecstatic relief of mutual assured responsibility, rancid fear forced fed pressed against angelic mouths; lips puckered, longing, sipping through savage ripe contagious acrimony. Taboos against blissful union. What happens when two beings of the same sex unite in an expansive ocean of flames? Burning away distance, psychosis, electrified doomsday barb wire fences; Titanic walls to keep screeching lovers treading their wheels. Dissolving into syrupy boozy ropes of precum charged with angst, sheets of sweat; A pliable transient sensation stretching beyond judgment of wanting this more than anything.

Do I embody the heroic masculine when I admit I've been responsible with my sexual dalliances? Is a *condom* something that compels, coaxes and invokes the supreme master of pleasure from the depths of our sexual potential?

Chained bound and broken, forced to suck tail pipe fumes of mediocrity. Dissociative acceptance letters tossed over rusted crumbling balconies into rank urine soaked cobble stone streets. Crowded inadequacies formed into brassy second line parades. Revved up writhing masses of lousy lovers, parasitic false alarms; early rising cataclysm. Putrid bubble atmosphere cradled in erosion. Acidic pricking torture genocide formed to hairline fracture. Narrow harrowing road of loneliness. Prison state of root and sacral center. Infinite vacuum loop of pious Latin chants raddling upward through ear canal. Infection. Lazy regurgitation lopsidedly crawling towards exorcism, subjective impositions, degradation. Incessant hammering against soft skull of new born abomination. Forking trident, grating steel. Tearing at itself, causing spine tingling reminders of the violence of lust.

One of us is destined to become the cleaver. The other will blossom, spread and ripen into the apple. Splitting exposure, breaking skin membrane to release pucker sweet juice only slick. *Never* truly wet. Accessible only through spearing reservoir of life force in bestial locking of horns. Steer boar bear. Frankenstein's doppelgänger.

What we birth from our congress... what we fuck to conceive, nurture and expand is a being of sexual nihilism. This energy can self-sustain on charred black landscape of dissolved structure. Self-penetrating sword. The inevitability of rawness.

11.
The Blossoming Alchemy of Arachne's Poisonous Architecture

Deliberate complexity. Silent suspension. A majestic fanning unfolding a multitude of masterfully skilled appendages. Steady ancient hands. Poised graceful threading. Straddling the divide between invitation and violation. Stiletto heels clanging like showers of lethal darts striking against tin shield, echoing ever closer through hollow canals of vertigo. The slimy tyrannical despot of seductive putrefaction. Arachne crawls oozing, through the thick fog; slimy satin sheets of sour vapor. Fleshy layers of resistance shrouding the hymen membrane between conscious and subconscious. Her fangs pierce to full penetration, aggressive resuscitation of creative potential within the human mind.

Tearing down well-worn posters you've outgrown from childhood through adolescence. Wall paper burning into air, the sigil of Lucifer draped like dusty velvet curtains around the true entry way. Nothing given only stolen, taken, in an act of sacred contravention. All arrows point inward, 6 drawn and 5 unseen narrowly laid through needle head. Pin point of desperate murderous desire to be accepted in. Dirty excrement ridden feet drag across pristine welcome mat.

Mammalian dive reflexing in a sea of poison. Self-soothing strangulation. Coughing up bloody cyclones of broken glass to finally wretch forth the beaten limp body of abomination. Expulsion initiated by icy orgasmic toxin of giant recluse spider biting down on big toe, hyper stimulation point. Rivulets of frost splash grappling hooks into fiery lava reservoirs of Draconian origin. Pressure between two extremes create misty waterfalls, portals of black and blue lagoons filled with strangers making love. Cresting above waves of labored humid exhales, rose gold oceans of creamy snot, oozing primitive forms of expression.

I'm the blossoming alchemy of Arachne's poisonous architecture.

Apple peach chemical gas burning faces and husks of skin. House of wax, house of horrors, house of whores; Belphegor. Raging currents of deep dead echoes, rotting wood. Wrought iron pole. Anger in the celebration of phallus fuck wand gallantly raping Smokey Pungent Earth.

An ash ridden wanderer emerges. Stagger stepping like a drunk hobo rambling insane spells. The fork in the road is the fork in his tongue. Circle walking the periphery of vestal terrain with a crooked shit eating grin plastered across a deviant midnight visage.

An unobstructed voyage has begun. Helium high elation. Anticipation of devastation.
The cyclical defilement of the most pure.

III.

Draconia Obscura, the Tightrope between Authenticity and Opportunity... or Malnourished Interests

I experience temporary relapse mourning the loss of belief systems that kept me fat, sick, ignorant and attuned to the common. Standing suspended on a creaky thin splintering rope bridge of isolation cradled in desolation. Muted screams in surround sound.

Sharp stabbing pangs release ever constrictive stitching. Dismantling a shrunken crude bodice. Antiquated jaundice thread snapping easily as she continues to rip and claw with maniacal focus, happily tearing away in complete silence. I can feel Arachne's poison surging adrenaline, flooding my bellicose nature. Battling to acidify the unbearable triplets of excess: thinking, sharing and allowing. Obstructive sadistic anxiety; conditioning, forced compulsion of staying in time, within the lines with just the right amount of words to comply. Slow motion breathy foreplay towards the erection of spontaneous ritual. Irresistible magnetism, lubed up motor oil wormwood bourbon cyanide. Sliding through strict narrow crawl spaces made of skin. Thick lipped schism reality. Positioning metallic sharp edged body as altar towards the twisted, sweet and sour sinister crooked fingered direction of SOUTHWEST. Sword tip pressed against the base of my spine. Diagonal line. Southeast gently dimmed itself to a faint iron vermillion. The muted softness of sanguine light and penetrative heavy feminine genius. A fleshy suctioning hive of tentacles anchoring hips and spearing anus, sliding body forward into the treacherous landscape ahead. Plunging belly flop onto chunky charcoal dust bowl. Atmosphere scraping away sensual engagement, fumbling around in a dark room looking for geometric clues. Horrible stars, flickering perpetual disappointment; lazily cast horizontal. A million hanged men mass Antichrist. Hollow continuum of sound arousing entry, chanting *ARACHNIDIA KA-RA-AN* quickly spinning out of control. Rambling babble blue note glossolalia formed to supremely unique spell casting. Wide winding dancer delicate shadow, brittle tattered shroud of crone shrinks to small insect giving tickling encouragement towards gripping of the Athame. White knuckled spartan grip with tremors of intentionally lopsided flopping; the bending of perfection to better suit mangled roads eroded away into venom filled bogs bubbling in tandem with my pulse.

Thick leathery wet Spider sack pushes through astral aperture, belching wisdom and raining black blood all over my naked body. She speaks casually; mentioning I should consider the coalescence between authenticity and opportunity. Visions of walking a brittle dry fraying tightrope flood my third eye as I attempt to understand the value and weight of this statement.

The following sentences should be spoken aloud:

How often do I create opportunities for myself to be authentic?

How often is it easier to assume a thought form or behavioral pattern of preconditioned prepackaged product for purchase?

Do I feed into the current of delusional mass formation psychosis?

The creation of space to express oneself in true autonomy is the most powerful and dangerous to birth. Its shape cements permanent fixture in the physical. It's a distinctive signature you can pull power from.

Light a black candle. Meditate with 11 Qliphothic shadow breaths and without hesitation, scratch your signature over a cheap flimsy piece of notebook paper. Put your blood on it. Burn the paper as you return to your inner psyche to envision the levitation of regality. Taking the obsidian throne with veins open, pouring rivers of black blood into deep chalices of the void. Feel Arachne spinning around your crown, pushing inwards to weave a design, a sigil; a shape. This is material for you to work with on the astral plane.

Waves of extreme relaxation like painful sharp but instantly euphoric novocaine blanket your auric bodies and release muscles, bones and tendons. Waterfalls of warm milk pearl alabaster with faint hue of iridescent aura pour from my heart, unlocked and open sprouting forth oasis. Paradise. A newborn version of the one who chooses not to take a name. Willing to toxify angelic brilliance with thick waves of contentment. The unwrapping of precious treasures. Flooding red skies with cloudy sour arrows to express the conscious choice to malnourish interests to feed action.

She won't drive you home and kiss you good night. She won't tell you everything's gonna be alright.

Spider Sorcery & the Black Sun

Edgar Kerval

The spider is a very important symbol in various ancient cultures around the world. In the hidden dynasties of ancient Egypt, the followers of the cult of Set worshipped a figure of Arachnean Goddess, and the magickal initiation into the cult involved using the venom of strange white spiders, which endowed the adept with the power of shape-shifting and traveling to unknown dimensions. It was also connected with the practice to walk into the desert in an invisible form with the purpose of performing necromantic rituals for those who crossed the line of time and space. The power of Archanean venom and its use as a powerful elixir to destroy or to heal is one of the most interesting subjects that can be explored in its many aspects through her many masks covered by her enigmatic mysticism. The spider is a powerful symbol of evolution, power and mystery.

Just as the spider weaves a web, we also have to weave our own path in the magickal initiation into her mysteries. Here, the Spider Goddess reveals to us the teaching of how each one of our actions can help us mold our life. As we progress through her hidden wisdom, we can explore the diverse paths and masks of her knowledge. Not only does the spider web teach us to draw our attention to our process of initiation into the path of sorcery but also gives us an overview of how our magickal perceptions and will can be mastered to build the magickal worlds we want to live in - we can achieve this by calling our primal consciousness to see the amazing construction of the spider's infernal and sempiternal web. This is the web of time and space, where all was formed and is still in transformation.

The spider symbol is associated with the symbol of the black sun. The spider has eight legs and eight eyes, and 8 is the number of black rays of infinity. However, we sometimes describe the Arachnean current with a totem of 12 rays, including the crossroads to her temples and the path with four ways. Each one of the paths offers us a different way of initiation. The main path is a black vortex opening to the influx of orgone and radiation energies surrounding our aura. The vibration frequency of the black sun, when it radiates its power onto the adept, indicates that the meaning of the number eight consists of cycles. It is the passages of time and evolution, which is experienced by the adept walking through the primal path of the Arachnean goddess.

The spider totem symbol calls on us to be mindful of how we explore the diverse paths and labyrinths of the Goddess, and to be receptive to the path of mysteries we weave from time to time. The transformative process within the Arachnean sorcery involves being consumed by the essence of the black sun and its primal rays as they are opening the vast paths of self-exploration to the adept. These 12 rays emerge as black light torches in the process of transcending beyond the progressive webs of the black Arachnean Goddess, becoming an instinctive totemic beast masked through the trees of divine madness. When the Arachnean

Goddess opens her eyes, an inner manifestation of her visions is transmitted through the path of initiation. The adept receives it through the primal language and through the fires burning beneath the hidden rays of the black sun.

When the adept explores the initiation process by focusing on the deepest mysteries of its hidden knowledge, sometimes it becomes raw and wild due its primal nature. Through this sinister alchemy the adept becomes ready to descend into the womb of the Goddess and to be the child in the egg, triggering a long and deep process of evolution. The deepest aspects of this initiation have their roots in the core of the adept's soul. They ignite a burning black flame that devours the essence of the adept and at the same time opens the womb of the Arachnean Goddess. The adept has to enlighten the path through darkness of his soul, which must be explored in order to transcend and to expand consciousness, focusing and channeling the sacred sexuality, arcane symbols, and deific masks, which are revealed when the adept disintegrates and purifies his soul.

In some ancient tribes, the spider was considered a powerful symbol of protection against storms and thunders. The spider as a totem is deeply connected with the way the universe evolves, and its movement is represented by time and space. It is also connected with the concept of the crone witch-mother, teacher, healer, and shamanic guardian of ancient esoteric wisdom, which is passed from ancestors to the next generations. The cosmic Arachnean Goddess of the universe is an integral part in this process, and she also appears in the myth of creation in the stories of many tribes.

In India, the spider is associated within the concept of Māyā and the veils of illusion. The term "Māyā" comes from the Sanskrit root "Ma," which means that there is no form or limit and describes the illusory nature of appearances and the destruction of the veils of all illusions in the mundane world. The association of the spider with Māyā brings us the understanding that not all things are as they appear to be, and prompts us to learn to see with the mental eye, with the eye of the spider, in order to learn how to "observe," "analyze" all elements and situations from the perspective of the depth.

In ancient Egypt, the spider is also associated with Neith, a complex deity usually represented with arrows and associated with creation of the universe, as well as with the concept of sunrise and sunset. Neith is also a weaver, and she is often shown holding a tool used for weaving. In ancient Greece, we have the Greek myth of Arachne, a mortal woman (although of noble birth), who was a spectacular weaver. Her fame for her skills with the looms spread through mountains and valleys and finally reached the ears of the immortal Athena.

The process of understanding the transition and initiation through the Arachnean mysteries is crowned in the final stage, when the adept transcends the veils of madness and destroys the illusion of Māyā. This can be achieved by focusing the essence of the black sun through invocation, using a circle formed by 12 stones and the Arachnean sigil representing the emanations of the black sun and each one of the 12 rays of spiritual transformation. This occurs under the eternal seal of the Arachnean Goddess, which moves backwards in order to clean and to bring the adept to the cycle of primal chaos, where the adept is now in the center of the throne of power, the one of the hidden tree, where the entrance is through Daath. The sinister path of the black sun opens its primal eye to converge in an eternal conjunction within the adept creating a potent primal union and awakening the powers of the depths when descending the vessels of Daath and drinking from the wisdom gathered through each emanation.

In a forest or wood, you must draw a big circle with 12 stones marked with drops of your own blood. Then you need to stand inside the circle with both arms pointing to the ground. After a deep meditation, invoke the chthonian force of the Arachnean Goddess with the purpose to awaken her powers within yourself. Dance backwards in spirals through the black sun circle to complete your purification, and after the ritual you shall rise as a new individual ready to explore other paths of the sinister Arachnean alchemy. Visualize the black sun rising from the ground, whose center is an opening eye, burning, surrounded by each one of its 12 emanations. Imagine black fire erupting its poisonous elixirs of purification upon you. Continue with the visualization until you feel the power emanating through all your being. Keep the stones for other future rituals and leave the place.

The Arachnean totem is a totem of primal wisdom. It invites us to transform our life from a higher magickal perspective and to see the cycles of death as rebirths which we explore through each one of the stages offered by its sacred gnosis. The spider is a totem of cunning, witchcraft and cyclic progression, rebirth and death, protection, and power over fate. Keep on exploring the 12 rays of the black sun through the webs of time and space of the Arachnean Goddess.

Spider Totem (Black Sun: 12 Rays of Transformation)

Conjuring the Spider Goddess
(Drinking from the Black Egg of the Void)

Edgar Kerval

Subterranean webs emerging through black holes
Veiled in madness and ecstasy
Arachnean primal totems erupting strange symbols
And vibrating through mantras of fire,
Under the stones of primogenial wisdom

Within the tincture of my soul,
The essence of my life,
And the seal of my mind,
I invoke you through the secret stone,
Through the hidden eye

Open the gates of your astral temple
And show me the path to follow,
Primal goddess of the shadows,
burn my soul to be reborn again,

under your primal light,
Oh, perpetual and invisible goddess of the void.

Open to me the secret path to cross the abyssal webs
And to drink from the black eggs,
Oh, great mother of the void
Devour me, and enlighten my path,
Through the hidden tunnels,
Reveal to me the secret key to cross the void eternally.

Through the black egg of vaporous visions
Come emanations of death trance mantras,
Evoking a secret temple, beyond the stars
Beyond the void of Arachnean webs.

Within the tincture of my soul,
The essence of my life,
And the seal of my mind,
I invoke you, Arachnean queen of death
through the secret stone,
Through your hidden eyes.

Open the gates of your astral temple
And show me the path to follow,
Primal goddess of the shadows,
burn my soul to be reborn again,
under your ineffable light,
Oh, perpetual and invisible goddess of space and time
Of the void and the sea of nothingness.

Spider Dream Oracle

Asenath Mason

When we look at the spider web, we see a structure of intricate patterns forming together a coherent whole. For this reason, since ancient times, the web has been the central part of many spiritual concepts and metaphorical theories. One of such concepts is the popular dreamcatcher. Perhaps you are familiar with its origins and symbolism, but if you are not, this article will introduce you to it, presenting a simple method to work with it in relation to the Spider Current.

I am sure you have seen a dreamcatcher, even if you do not use it yourself. Modern dreamcatchers usually look like a hoop with a design woven in the form of a spider's web, and they have beads or feathers hanging from it. They are often beautiful, made from various materials, embellished with crystals, gems, and other jewelry pieces. They can be small, meant to hang above the bed, or they are big and put on the walls as decorations. Originally, dreamcatchers did not have feathers or beads and were simple in design. Today, you can find dreamcatchers in many different sizes and embellishments, but the basic concept behind them is still the same – they imitate a spider's web and its mystical qualities.

What are these qualities? We have already talked about the meaning of the spider's web many times in this book. There are, however, certain things characteristic for the dreamcatcher. The circular shape is often believed to represent a cycle - this can be the cycle of life, death, rebirth, or simply the cycle of life - from birth, through childhood and adulthood, to elderly age and death. Sleep is an important part of our life cycle. We spend 1/3 of our lives sleeping. The realm of dreams is therefore just as important to us as our waking reality, and dream analysis has been the subject of studies from ancient times. The role of the dreamcatcher in the science of dreaming seems simple - it is believed to filter good and bad dreams, those that are pure fantasy and those that carry insights about ourselves, dreams produced by our mind and those sent by gods and spirits to guide us in our life. The web is a trap for unwanted dreams - it stops them from happening, allowing only those that are good and beneficial for us. Sometimes it is believed that the feathers and beads hanging from the circle are the dreams that were caught in the web and transformed into more positive forms.

To understand the idea behind the dreamcatcher, though, we have to look back at its origins and the traditional meaning. The image of the dreamcatcher is derived from the Native American culture, and to be more specific, it originated among the Ojibwa people. In their language, the word for the dreamcatcher was "asabikeshiinh," which translates to "spider." There is also a legend that explains how it came into being, which involves the figure of the Spider Woman. According to the story, the Ojibwa once lived in one area called the Turtle Island. At that time, the Spider Woman protected them as her people. When the tribe dispersed to the four corners of the North America, she could no longer travel to all of them, and so the women started weaving magical webs, imitating the web of the Spider Woman, to protect their families. Traditionally, the dreamcatchers were hung over a bed or cradle and believed to let the good dreams flow and catch the bad dreams, hold them, and keep them away from the person they protected. The small circle within the bigger one in the dreamcatcher was the point where the good dreams and thoughts entered the mind of the sleeping. Then, with the first rays of sunlight, the Spider Woman would destroy the bad dreams caught up in the web. For this reason, the original dreamcatchers, as well as most modern ones, had eight points where the web in the center connected to the hoop, representing the number of the spider legs. Sometimes, a feather was placed in the center as well, to represent the breath of air and the life-giving power of the goddess. This tradition is sometimes retained and appears in modern dreamcatchers as well.

As we can see, there is a direct connection between the dreamcatcher and the Spider Current, and although many practitioners discard working with such symbols because of their appearance in popular culture, I believe it is worth exploring as the idea behind the object is old and can still be interesting to work with, especially in regard to Gnosis of the Spider.

There are many interpretations of the dreamcatcher symbolism, just as there are many speculations on the metaphorical meaning of the spider web. Usually, we meet with the idea that the object allows good dreams pass through it and stops the bad ones. However, another idea is that a dreamcatcher placed above the bed of a sleeping person catches good dreams and lets them slide down into the mind of the sleeper, ensuring calm and peaceful sleep filled with beautiful visions, while the bad dreams pass through it and dissipate. As we see, there is more than one way to work with it, and it leaves an interesting field to explore for a practitioner working with the Spider Current.

Another interpretation focuses on the various meanings of the dreamcatcher's design. Each part of it is important and nothing is random. Originally, dreamcatchers were made from natural materials, usually willow. Today, we can meet with a variety of materials, from natural and based on plants to synthetic, or even involving metal, like in jewelry. The circular shape of the dreamcatcher represents the sun and its movement across the sky - from the east to the west. At the center is the pattern of threads typifying the spider's web, with a small hole that was originally believed to let the good dreams travel through, while the bad ones were trapped in the net. The web itself was supposed to catch the first rays of sunlight in the morning, which were believed to destroy the nightmares and evil spirits that were trapped in it throughout the night. The feather inside the web represented air, breath, the life-giving force. The ones hanging from the hoop were either symbolic of the dreams transformed through the power of the spider's web or they had an additional protective function. Some people would say that they provided a distraction to nightmares and malicious spirits visiting a sleeping person, thus protecting them from being haunted or possessed. Gemstones are a later invention and did not appear in the original designs. Today their meaning and function depends on the kind, color, and their magical properties, and we can construct a dreamcatcher reflecting our intent and program the crystals to empower it. This is what we will be dealing with in the following ritual.

The working presented below is based on the meaning of the dreamcatcher in connection to the symbolism of the spider's web. What this symbolism includes depends largely on the context and the culture/religion. In some parts of the world the spider is a feared animal as its bites are painful and its venom is deadly. In others, it is a symbol of wisdom, creativity and luck. It has as many positive as negative meanings. What we work with when we enter the path of the Spider is this ambiguity, the multiplicity of symbols and interpretations. We also learn how to be a spider and stand in the center of the web, how to move through it freely, instead of being entangled in the threads and end up as a victim of fate. If we get caught in the web of the Spider Goddess, like a fly, we eventually become consumed with fear and unable to move forward, struggling with the life circumstances but never attempting to change them and overcome the obstacles. Instead, we become passive observers of our life, missing out the opportunities for growth. The circular shape of the spider's web represents the wheel of life, the karmic cycle, presenting us with the multiplicity of possible futures and outcomes of our actions. The Spider Goddess teaches us that it is possible to influence and manipulate the wheel and change the cycle, to weave the thread of our life as we want it. While working with the dreamcatcher symbol in connection with the Spider Current we learn how to let the things we want into our life and stop the others from entering, how to choose what we live and how we live it instead of simply accepting life circumstances as they come.

The spider is a creator. It weaves the design of life and destiny - from the beginning to the end. This work is cyclic and never-ending - if the web is damaged or destroyed, it weaves it anew. However, the spider is also a destroyer. It traps its victims until they are dead and leaves their corpses to decay. For this reason, it typifies fear, especially the fear of death. Arachnophobia is very common among people, and it has also been the theme for many books and horror movies. This ambiguity of the spider symbolism allows us to use it to confront certain issues in ourselves, such as phobias and insecurities, the fear of the future and inability to move forward when we get stuck in the day-to-day struggles. The Spider Goddess shows us that suppressing these issues is not a solution, and that they will always, sooner or later, come up to the surface. It is for a reason that she is the force presiding over the Qliphothic labyrinths, confronting the traveler to the Nightside with all kinds of nightmares and manifestations of "inner darkness." She is as benevolent as ruthless and lethal. On the other hand, this ambiguity gives us additional insights into what we need to change in ourselves - what has to be improved and what should rather be left behind. Therefore, one of her lessons is maintaining balance - between conscious and unconscious, past and future, physical and spiritual. She teaches us to stand in the center of all of it, looking at our life from the perspective of the weaver of fate. She can show us how to weave our dreams and fantasies into reality, how to focus on our goals and enjoy our accomplishments, and how to move toward the chosen direction instead of being pulled in many others.

The ritual presented here involves the idea that dreams can be used as an oracle. This is an ancient concept, and in the past the art of interpreting dreams was known as oneiromancy, from the Greek words *oneiros* (dream), and *manteia* (prophecy). Ancient people believed that dreams may be used to prophesy the future, look into the past and explain the cause of the events happening in the present, and to provide an advice on how a person should act in a particular situation. Sometimes the practices of oneiromancy were accompanied by certain herbs and psychoactive potions or ointments to induce dream-like states of consciousness. The oracle was the sleeping person, who, upon waking up, would deliver the message revealed in a dream to those who came with questions. In the following working, we will use the elements of oneiromancy as well. For this, you have to create your own dreamcatcher. You can also purchase one if you are really not good with crafts, but a dreamcatcher made with your own hands will work better. If possible, use natural materials and feathers, and decorate the item with pieces of amethyst. You can also use a different crystal, but amethyst is believed to have a natural connection to your third eye, and thus to your subconscious mind. I recommend natural crystals and not just plastic beads because crystals can be programmed, and this is exactly what we will do in our ritual.

When your dreamcatcher is ready, you can proceed to the ritual itself. You will also need a few black candles, the sigil of Arachne (you can use the sigil provided on page 36), and some strong incense - wormwood, dragon's blood, copal, etc. Place it all on the altar, together with the dreamcatcher, and begin the ritual. One piece of amethyst should be left loose. You will then place it under the pillow or keep it next to your bed as a point of connection to the energies of the Spider Goddess.

Light the candles, burn some incense, and focus for a moment on the sigil of the Spider Goddess to activate it. Anoint it with your blood, and place a drop of it on your forehead, in the area of the third eye, as well as on the dreamcatcher. Then focus on invoking the Spider Goddess and assuming the "spider consciousness." Such practices are described in some of my books, e.g., in *Tunnels of Set*. If you do not have experience with that, however, simply focus on the sigil while chanting the mantra: "Arachnidia Ka-Ra-An." When you see that the sigil responds to your chanting and starts to glow and morph into other shapes, recite the following words of consecration. You can also replace them with your own.

Arachne, Spider Goddess, hear my calling and answer it!
I call you into my temple, my body, and my mind!
Charge this dreamcatcher with your timeless essence,
Make it alive and make it your dwelling place,
Let it catch the dreams that are filled with your gnosis,
And stop the ones that are not relevant to my growth,
Let the sunlight destroy them!
Fill my dreams with visions of what I need to know,
Send them to me through the crystals and the feathers,
Show me how to use what I receive from you,

And do not let me forget what I learn through my dreaming visions!

At the same time, feel the energy flowing through the sigil enter your body and penetrate your mind. Focus on this feeling for a while and see what it is like to be a spider - how you can look at your life from the perspective of the center and what insights may come to you then.

Dreams sent by the Spider Goddess show how the various events and situations from your life connect together, and how you are connected to different people appearing on your path. She helps you see the invisible connections, providing insights into your actions and choices, past and future - as she also shows that everything is cyclic. She may also bring the suppressed thoughts, emotions, or traumas to the surface to facilitate emotional healing. For many people painful situations can be transformative in a negative way - they may produce fear and trauma that makes them withdraw from the world in an attempt to avoid getting hurt more. As a consequence, they may become focused on the negativity of life, giving in to self-pity and unable to enjoy anything. By working with the Spider Goddess, we are shown the cause of our traumas and the reason why we react to them the way we do. If you program the dreamcatcher to filter the negativity, you will be able to look at the "bad" experiences in your life without emotional attachment and find a way to resolve them or at least transform the pain into peace and strength. Like a vacuum, the dreamcatcher will absorb and then destroy the negative associations and emotional burden, allowing you to find the joyful side of life and put your mind at ease. To make it happen, focus on the crystals in the dreamcatcher and will them either to absorb and store the negativity or to catch the positive energy and store it for you. This is entirely up to you. In the first case, you will need to hang the dreamcatcher in the place exposed to sunlight, and each morning "tell" the crystals to cleanse themselves with the sun rays. In the latter case, you can either will the crystals to transmit the positive energy to you automatically, or you can meditate on the dreamcatcher each morning to absorb this force. Do not forget to program the loose crystal, too. For this, simply keep it in your projecting hand, focusing on the intent to make it a point of connection between you and the dreamcatcher. Then keep it next to you at night.

While working with the Spider Goddess through dreams it is important to keep a dream journal and write down all dream visions, no matter if they seem "magical" or "mundane." It is often through the simple, mundane symbols that the most profound messages are conveyed. Another important thing is to meditate on what these dreams may mean and how they relate to your questions and growth opportunities. It is very unlikely that the answer to what you seek will come to you in a direct way. What you should expect are dreams covering the answer by means of metaphors and allegories. Pay attention to the places you visit in your dreams, the characters you interact with, and the situations you face - all these may carry a message for you, granting a new perspective on your life and providing guidance when you need it. This is a long-term work, so be patient and approach it with an open mind and a great deal of dedication. Do not forget to cleanse your dreamcatcher regularly. Otherwise, it may store the negativity and keep the unwanted entities trapped, instead of releasing them and acting as a proper conductor between you and the Spider Current.

Autism and Immortality:
Variations on a Theme by Ovid

Denerah Erzebet

In Ovid's original account, Arachne was a mortal woman. Therefore, she is not the original identity of the spider goddess we honor in the Draconian Tradition. Conveniently, she is a familiar face from a more recent epoch, namely: ancient Greek civilization. In this context, I consider early Greek society "recent" or *relatable* in terms of having established the foundation of Western values. Notably, we find among their works the template for our modern democracy and clearly divided "nation-states." Likewise, several assumptions of a metaphysical nature are subconsciously accepted by most people today - and if not accepted, they are fiercely debated among philosophers, artists and theologians. Finally, the ethical inquiries of Plato and Aristotle are nearly taken for granted, often filtered through Christian perspectives in the works of medieval scholars such as Thomas Aquinas.

Thus, it is no surprise that occultism would also borrow from a tradition whose major works have survived in a complete form, and given credible assessment. Even in "new age" religions such as Wicca, we observe a tendency to invoke pagan deities in their Greek form, rather than through Babylonian, Egyptian, or European reflections (at least up until recent decades, when deeper archeological and scholarly interpretations have surfaced). Perhaps it is also due to the essentially *human* portrayals of Hellenic gods, rather than the earlier anthropomorphic forms, that engender sympathy on our part.

Actually, I myself find the Egyptian deities rather abstract in comparison to European embodiments of the same animistic forces. Of course, no pagan tradition is truly equivalent - being refractions of cosmic laws into several forms endowed with the ethnic, ancestral, and cultural preferences of their devotees. For this reason, I consider "equivalent gods" as offering different aspects of the same archetype. Perhaps our Western gods are more intimate manifestations of elemental power (lust, warfare, fertility, etc.), while Egyptian deities represent the intellectual dimension of nature crafted through geometry, architecture, and astronomy.

Likely, these may be the motivations behind sorcerers adopting Arachne as a placeholder name for an essentially nameless archetype - the Spider who weaves the primordial substance into distinct forms, and whose venom paralyses such offspring in her web of fate.

After all, the Nameless Chaos can only be known through its manifest forms, when it becomes *something* of particular significance. Animism thus advocates for insight through tangible phenomenon, cooperating with the senses rather than denying them.

This is the premise upon which "Instinctive Iconography" is established, whose furthest abstraction is but Erotic Geometry, in the manner of Plato's world of Ideal Forms (see *The Eleventh Degree*). However, these are still forms, no matter how perfect, because the Unknowable cannot be known beyond such crude symmetry. In this case, the Image in Flesh is God or Goddess, or Entity clothed in cultural tendencies, while Geometry is the Formula or Eternal Principle (Archetype) behind the Goddess, the "atomic denominator" assuming various forms refracted from this same, timeless principle. For instance, every pantheon from Egypt to Sweden has a "fertility goddess," names and myths are the embodiment of "fertility" itself, as understood by mortals through immediate recognition of their natural surroundings.

From the imagery of myth we strive for the allegory of cosmic law. This equally applies to Arachne, whose tale permits a greater comprehension of the Spider-principle discussed in the previous essay (*Our Lady of Silk and Space*).

Let us therefore examine Arachne's legend, as told by Ovid in *Metamorphoses*. Her story occurs specifically in Book VI, from whose pages I now paraphrase:

Minerva (goddess of wisdom) tore Arachne's disgraceful tapestry to pieces, cursing her to morph into the Spider-Totem and weave without respite. Clearly, she was displeased with Arachne's blatant depiction of immoral behavior among the gods of Olympus. Through an honest endeavor to expose Zeus and Neptune's numerous acts of rape, adultery, and promiscuity, she channeled the timeless "obsession" for truth, so that her *eternal form* involves ceaseless weaving, spinning, and crafting (an ironic and fitting punishment on Minerva's part).

Likewise, our own immortality is based upon "obsessional drives" here and now on earth. A musician will likely become a Hermes or Apollo, whereas a veterinarian or environmentalist may become a nymph or land spirit serving Artemis or Ceres. That which we are not, defines us, in the sense that STRIVING establishes our eternal image on the astral plane. For instance, one doesn't "see" Mozart centuries later as anything but a prolific genius completing over 600 works in 35 years. His perpetual pattern is to write music.

This gives us a chance to decide now what we will be forevermore - success in terms of public recognition or wealth isn't of value to the Gods - so long as we *create obsessively* with no consideration for fame and fortune. As long as we adhere to a relentless routine, we shall immortalize ourselves! This is because *something greater* inspires us, and to create art as an end in itself is actually filled with the greatest purpose: pleasing the Deity who inspires us, the Immortal Beloved behind all our desires, hopes, ambitions, and dreams.

Rigorous and repetitive activity is often considered a symptom of Autism, when an individual classed on the autistic "disorder" spectrum seems compelled to execute a highly detailed routine without respite. In fact, several autistic types experience acute emotional anxiety when they are asked to modify the quality or order of their daily activities. To outsiders, a mere change of time appears harmless, while *devoted Changelings* will rebel against "music listening" having to begin at noon instead of the *proper* 11 am.

I intend now to stress that I do not consider autistic tendencies as a "disorder" needing treatment at the hands of scientific orthodoxy, nor do I uphold absolute trust in today's prevailing materialism. Furthermore, I insist on classifying "outsiders" as anyone who stands apart from another's worldview, which equally applies to "autistic" children in regard to a "neurotypical" mentality. I've written before that *we are all an-other to one another*, mere incapacity for immersion in another's subjective framework makes us all outsiders to diverging ideas.

For this reason, and none other, I stand apart from both contemporary ethics and positive science.

Formerly, autistic behavior in children was a sure sign that they were *not human*, or rather hailing from *some other world*. Often, these were signs that the Faery Folk cunningly replaced a human infant with one of their own. Since Faeries match our physical features, only behavioral traits could properly identify a Changeling among our ranks. Indeed, social "ineptitude" exhibited by autistic children was explained as follows: Changelings carry, in their souls, the customs of Faery society, which seems more idyllic and just than our own, and cannot cope with a species driven by greed, lust, violence, and hypocrisy. In addition, artistic and spiritual pursuits are deemed "unnecessary" here, while the Fae praise them as *true and timeless beauty* (being immortal and therefore immune to biological needs).

Many of these statements have been confirmed by the spirits, Fae or otherwise, that I am fortunate to behold.

Thus, the Spider Queen (as Arachne) becomes a matron and totem for all who feel an "inexplicable" urge to create, craft, and contemplate all that human need considers "superfluous" and "non-essential!"

I salute all fellow Changelings, who would rather relinquish this mortal body than merely subsist in a world devoid of true purpose...*our purpose!*

This accounts for the elemental aspect of the arachnidian strain. The second aspect, *the Spider Queen of Space*, serves as the celestial counterpart to the Faery Folk.

If Changelings are the necessary *cure* for a hopelessly human paradigm, then we may also classify alien intrusions as "poisons" to a merely terrestrial, carbon-based life. (For preliminary understanding of "poison gnosis," please consult my essay *Lady of Silk and Space*.)

The Faery Folk inspire the soul through poetry and music, while celestial beings oversee our genetic and biological mutation. The former, being "another side" of earth, work with *fantastic forms* to enchant our senses, while alien star-souls help us overcome physical limitations in order to manifest the perfection we idolize (in works of art).

In Ovid's account, it is written: "She [Pallas/Minerva] sprinkled Arachne with the juice of Hecate's herb. Immediately, at the touch of this baneful poison, the girl's hair dropped out... Her whole body, likewise, became tiny... Her slender fingers were fastened to her sides... And as a spider is busy with her web as of old." (Ovid, *Metamorphoses*, translated by Mary M. Innes, Penguin Books, 1955).

Here we have explicit mention of substances causing magical transformation - in this case attributed to Hecate as the Goddess of Witchcraft. A liberal interpretation offers us insights into the dynamic interaction between terrestrial and celestial *influences*, which I expect will incite further reflection:

Arachne already knew what the gods were doing, so to speak. Many of the victims were nymphs (Faery/Sprite) so Arachne already possessed insight regarding secret plots, motivations, and movements of cosmic forces. In other words, her soul had seen beyond the veil. All that was left to achieve was the immortal embodiment of her devotion - an external poison was necessary to effect a complete transformation. Likewise, no true mutation of the human race can be achieved by "technology" alone... We rely on a Higher Authority to administer the "fatal dose..."

This is where our understanding emerges of Alien Races coming *in* from outer space, or likewise, *radiating through the apparatus of celestial "bodies."* One must remember that they are not physical inhabitants of some other planet like we, otherwise they wouldn't be capable of withstanding space travel at light speed, among other crucial limitations of carbon-based life. Instead, they use some distant planet or star as an "anchor" to *imagine themselves to us.* This is their application of "mythic imagery" previously discussed. Furthermore, specific names are selected with a conscious knowledge of religious and esoteric correspondences. Such *lenses* are used to reveal their nature refracted through anthropology and myth. Thus, one race will present themselves as hailing from Orion and another from Cassiopeia, in order to distinguish their individual natures.

We see this approach reflected in the presentation of "starseed" souls in several New Age circles, wherein various stars and galaxies embody specific personality traits, and are held accountable for natural psychics, empaths, and *Changeling behavior.* This is but another reflection of the dynamic between spirit and matter occurring here on earth. Instead of spirit, we may call it radiation or star dust - to them it is truly immaterial.

The complex network of galaxies is but the spider's web above - or better still, *around* this small point we call Earth. Truly, our stance is equally somewhere else to them, all things *even* under the Spider's watchful gaze.

Weaver of Fate

David Weaver

I had no idea I would be writing an essay for the Arachne anthology for the Temple of Ascending Flame until this morning after I awoke from an unsettling dream featuring a large banana spider sitting in the center of its web oh-so-sinisterly in my bicycle helmet, presumably waiting to devour my brain or perhaps even my soul. When I saw the Temple was doing an anthology for Arachne and inviting members to contribute, I thought to myself "No, that's not for me, I'm not ready to work with Arachne in depth." Why? Frankly, she terrifies me. Of all the gods, goddesses and spirits I have encountered on the Dragon's path so far, none terrify me the way she does, and, here's the kicker: I'm not even afraid of spiders! Not in the mundane sense, anyway. I'm actually quite fond of spiders. In fact, I love spiders! I allow them free range of my dwelling and never make any attempt to remove or relocate them. They're welcome inhabitants, and I actually enjoy having a few spiders just casually hanging out in my room above my bed in the corners of the room.

I've not always been so unafraid of spiders, however, and, at a primal level, if I'm honest, I'm still very much terrified of them. Sounds complicated, right? Well, that's where the magick of the Spider Queen comes into play. Not everything is as it seems on the surface. Her mysteries are deep. In my experience, her lessons and messages are almost never on the conscious or mundane level of existence, although they often can and do manifest in our mundane lives as real experiences and trials. In this respect, she effectively weaves together Nightside and Dayside.

While on the surface, in my waking state, during the sunlight hours, I can hang out with spiders all day and be completely at ease (I am totally fascinated with everything having to do with spiders: how they weave their webs - what works of art! The geometry! How patient they are in waiting for their prey, so still and silent as they do - if only I could have a fraction of that patience in my own life how far that could go! Have you ever seen spiders fly? You mean you didn't know spiders can fly? Well, they can!), at night, in the darkest hours when I'm what's for dinner, when I'm that piece of meat writhing in fear and trepidation at the center of her web waiting to be devoured, it's a whole different story!

So, my relationship with spiders in the mundane world is more likened to that of an admiring and fascinated naturalist, whereas, my relationship with them and their corresponding Queen in a magickal sense is horrifying, cold and deadly in every sense of the word. I don't say this to discourage anyone from working with her (that is something that each practitioner must decide for themselves), I simply mean to relay my personal experience in the hopes that others may find some useful insight on their own journey, and, if you're on the fence about working with her and just want to know more, what one could expect in general. That being said, your results may differ greatly from mine or anyone else's, but the themes remain similar.

In a nutshell, the themes and keywords in working with the Spider Queen include but are not limited to: shadow work, poison, traumatic experiences, transformation, death, renewal, our own sinister and predatory nature, primal instincts, dreams, the unconscious mind, buried memories, unresolved conflicts both intra and interpersonal, weaving our own web, creating our fate, plotting the demise of our prey, psychopathic personality traits we have but may be unwilling to admit or accept, creative genius, stillness, patience, lurking in the dark, fear, feminine nature, travel. Also, any associations that can be made with actual spiders are appropriate. If a particular breed of spider stands out to you above all others, then that means there is something particular about that spider which has something to offer you. In what ways is it unlike other spiders? What makes it unique?

Arachne's mysteries penetrate to the darkest parts of the self, the catacombs of the psyche - that dark and mysterious place hidden deep within us all, the forgotten and disregarded past, as well as the uncertain and unknown future that lies ahead. The place that contains all our secrets, all our unresolved conflicts, all our unintegrated personality traits, and all those parts of ourselves that we would deny emphatically that we have, and by working with Arachne all of those things will be brought to the surface. Everything you think you've hidden from yourself or forgotten about will be rolled out. Every undigested and unprocessed piece of trauma, every unresolved internal and external conflict (intrapersonal and interpersonal) will be rolled out from deep within her lair like a wolf spider rolling out a kill from days long forgotten, to be unwrapped, analyzed and devoured.

A word of caution to those seeking to work with the Spider Queen: you will be forced to confront the darkest parts of yourself, and her trials are not to be taken lightly. Her tests can end in insanity or death, if failed, and a renewed self full of vitality, purpose and freedom you've never known, if passed. In other words, the stakes are high. Her venom poisons and kills the mundane self and world in a cold and ruthless manner, but they're always things that must die in order for us to grow and evolve on our path as the weavers of our own fate. In this way, she liberates us from our fears and limitations through direct and brutal confrontation with them.

Everything you've tried to unsuccessfully kill, bury and forget, the corpses will be dredged up, carried out from the depths of your psyche and laid bare for you to examine, and you must be prepared for this to manifest in the mundane world, too (so, if you're literally a serial killer with buried corpses hanging about, perhaps this is work you'd rather avoid if you wish to remain a free man or woman. Joking, joking! Or am I?). The corpses of your past, any unpleasant experience you have not processed, digested or allowed may present as rotting corpses infested with black, necrotic fluid, their faces gaunt and frozen in terror, eyes wide. Her venom can not only kill, bringing a quick and merciful death, it can also paralyze and keep us alive in situations where death would seem a merciful alternative. These corpses she brings forth are the traumatized and fragmented pieces of our psyche that Arachne can help us to restore. Her healing is like no other. It may be advisable to have a counselor or psychologist of some sort to help work through the buried pains of the past, but in the end, it's not so much about "working through" it as much as it is embracing these parts of our self and accepting them as part of who and what we are.

No essay on Arachne would be complete without discussing her silvery, silken web. She is the spinner of fate, and when we invoke her essence, we become the weaver of our own destiny. Suddenly, we are held 100% accountable for all the connections we've spun into our web: every place and person we've been is contained in this web as well as all the people and places we will be; and, we're the ones who built it.

In this way, she teaches the initiate personal accountability and reminds us that our destiny is our own to shape. Since we're the ones who built the web we find ourselves in, that means we alone can also destroy and alter it, remake it however we so choose.

Just as quickly as we've added something to our web, it can be cut out and cast into the Abyss. Speaking from personal experience, it's not easy to remove an attachment, especially when there is such a strong emotional need associated with it. That's where Arachne teaches us to be like her for our own benefit and evolution: to have a cold and sinister approach to those things in our life that no longer serve us well or have already fulfilled their purpose in our story and need to be released. In this process of releasing things from our life, a little bit of compassion and gratitude go a long way in bringing a sense of completion, acceptance and thankfulness for the role these things played in our life, but if that feeling of warmth for those things prohibits us from letting them die and keeps us from moving on and evolving when we need to, we must sacrifice our empathy for them in order to do what we must so that we can transform.

At first glance, she can appear terrifying and unapproachable, but her gift is the deepest form of healing we can experience - the healing of our soul. It is a painful and difficult process and anyone who says "yeah, I worked with the Spider Queen, underwent a complete transformation of my soul with her and it was easy, no trials or hardships whatsoever, by far the breeziest walk in the park yet!" was more likely working with a delusion of their own grandeur than an actual manifestation of her. All jokes aside, pursuing the attainment of the Spider Queen's gnosis is like courting our own poisoning, death and renewal. This in itself can be a terrifying experience and manifest in our daily lives as the loss of illusions regarding relationships we're in, associations we have, jobs we work, tasks we perform, and quests we pursue.

If you're ready to allow her venom to transform you at the deepest level, or even if you aren't ready, the Spider Queen could be the one you're looking for, but chances are that if you've gone so far as to buy this book and read this essay, she already has you in her web. *cue sinister music*

Jorogumo, Black Widow Spiders and Black Widow Women

Last night, before falling asleep, I asked the Spider Queen to guide my dreams about how to proceed with writing part two of this essay, and she responded. At first, I thought I would create a ritual working to complement part one until I realized that part one was not complete as an essay, so here we are. That being said, I may still publicly release ritual workings I author at a later date so stay tuned for that if you wish. Now let's dive in, shall we?

In Japanese folklore, there is a tale of a being known as the Jorogumo. There is much information about this entity already available so I will not try to add to its compendium as I know very little of the actual history behind this myth, so I will not pretend to be an expert on the Jorogumo because what is most poignant here is the archetype of this myth: that of a seductive young woman who lures men into bed before transforming into a spider and eating them. This archetype spans well beyond the borders of Japan and I believe the Jorogumo is a cultural mask of a much greater collective archetype that can be found in many cultures and myths around the world. In my opinion, the Jorogumo is indeed a mask of the Spider Queen.

Now I would like to compare the Jorogumo to a contemporary Western archetype: that of the black widow. In Western culture, a "black widow" (aside from being an incredibly cool spider that we'll be discussing later) is used as a nickname to refer to a flesh-and-blood human woman who I believe embodies the essence of the Spider Queen in all her horror. Much like the black widow spider she is nicknamed after, she has a tendency to murder and eat her lovers post-coitus. While there are some obvious differences between the black widow woman and the black widow spider, their instincts, motivation and nature are nearly identical when examined closely, and, again, I believe that both are physical manifestations of the Spider Queen.

If you've never watched a documentary video about the mating habits of black widow spiders, now is a good time to catch up: it's truly fascinating! In a nutshell, courting is extremely dangerous for the male black widow spider. It's literally a life-and-death decision when a male black widow spider decides to mate. In choosing to pursue the act of procreation, he is placing himself on the altar of sacrifice. At an instinctual level, the male must know that he could well be eaten once the act of mating is complete because once the deed is done, the male has one thing on his mind: the exit! It's a get in and get out as quick as he can operation, and for good reason! The longer he sticks around, the greater the chance he will be eaten. The smart ones jet immediately after intercourse, and I mean *immediately*. If he's lucky, if he's fast enough, or if perhaps his mistress is feeling merciful that day, he will escape and live to breed another day. From an evolutionary perspective, this ensures that only the fittest and fastest males are able to breed more than once and therefore have more offspring.

Where is all this going? So glad you asked. Take everything you just learned about black widow spiders and apply it to human nature. In what ways are we similar? Modern cultural attitudes like to pretend that we are "above" such primitive instincts, but I can assure you from personal experience and careful observation of human behavior that we most certainly are not. Let's not kid ourselves and have a mature conversation about the mating habits, sexual instincts and primal desires of our human selves, brothers and sisters, shall we? I realize that I run the risk of pissing some people off by addressing what I'm about to address and blowing the carefully crafted covers of others, but I've weighed the pros and cons thoroughly and decided it's much more beneficial to continue.

Black widow women are similar to black widow spiders in that they have a tendency to kill their mates, only in this case, she doesn't necessarily cannibalize her prey's corpse, but instead inherits (or steals, depending on how you want to look at it) the man's wealth. Black widows typically target wealthy men with the intent to seduce, marry, murder, and steal all his worldly possessions (in that order) - everything he's worked for, everything he's expended his energy on and earned during the course of his life. It is an extreme and primal form of predation that, at its core, I believe serves a useful function: that of ensuring the survival of the species, but when misdirected or unacknowledged by either party, can result in the stuff of nightmares and you'll never see it coming.

This is the part where I compare humans to spiders. You see, we like to kid ourselves and pretend that men serve a function beyond the utility of providing genetic material to the female and acquiring resources for his offspring to ensure their chances of survival and thus his version of carnal immortality, which he receives in exchange for all his sacrifice, but in the natural order of things he does not. In the natural order of things, the man's usefulness does not extend beyond providing sperm and material resources to the queen (and by queen I mean his wife, partner, lover, or even just the random encounter with a one-night-stand at the bar). In effect, the male sacrifices his life for the future of his species and it's not much more complicated than that. If he fails to provide utility to the queen either via genetic material in the form of sperm, or bringing her material resources, then the only resource he can provide is his own body and the nutrition it provides. It's a dangerous game we play with each other, and if not taken seriously, can result in dire consequences for both parties, so let's keep it real.

As a heterosexual man who was misguided about men, women and how we relate, I had to figure out everything for myself in the harshest ways possible: through direct and brutal encounters with the Spider Queen. I've walked blindly into her lair on more than one occasion, believing I was headed to the Disney World of every boy's romantic fantasy and it nearly cost me my life. In fact, I barely walked away with my sanity intact (despite losing it several times) and had to work for years in order to regain much of it. Some days I look back and think "how did I survive that?!"

Thanks to the gnosis of the Spider Queen, I have begun to make peace with the horrors of my past and have gained a healthy respect and even admiration of female nature, the natural world, human women, my encounters with them and my relationship to them in the process. I've seen men go the complete opposite direction, myself temporarily included: becoming jaded, resentful, full of hostility and rage towards women - all stemming from a foundational misunderstanding of female nature and my relationship to them as a man. I still have much to learn. In short, the Spider Queen can heal both men and women, helping them to better understand their nature and come to terms with who and what we are at the most primal level, but such trials are never easy. Results will vary from person to person as we're all in different phases of our evolution, so what the Queen of Spiders has to teach you may look nothing like what she taught me.

I'd also like to take this opportunity to put to rest the myth that you have to perform rituals or be a magickian in order to attract the attention of the Spider Queen and undergo her trials. Long before I ever heard about Arachne or performed a single ritual as a self-identified magickain, I was tangled in her web undergoing her trials. That being said, I have found that formally working with her and intentionally fostering a relationship with her in my magickal practice to be intensely rewarding. While I've spared the most personal details of my story in this particular essay, it is among other things a cautionary tale of walking into another spider's web and harnessing our own creative powers to focus on weaving our own. Arachne teaches us to be the spinners of our own web. Acknowledging and respecting the webs of others, proceeding with caution, avoiding getting wrapped up in another spider's silk by focusing on our own, and dropping all naivete about our primal, sinister nature have been primary themes regarding my gnosis of the Spider Queen thus far.

In what ways can you look back and recognize Arachne's thread woven through your life without your notice? If your relationship with her is anything like mine, she's been with you the entire time - with subtle signs of her presence all around, always lurking, never far. Hail Arachne! Hail the Spider Queen!

The Spider Goddess of the Labyrinth

Darío G.

*"Where is Ariadne's thread to guide me
out of dangerous Scylla, out of this stable of Augeas?"*[*]

We become familiar with labyrinths from a very young age. Sometimes we have contact with them or knowledge of them through magazines, games or hobbies in the kindergarten, or at school. These patterns of paths and complex designs have been drawn from a few thousand years ago to the present day. The best known to all of us is the labyrinth of King Minos, a labyrinth that was built by Daedalus with the purpose of imprisoning the Minotaur, a terrifying creature with the head and tail of a bull and the body of a man, who ate humans for food. According to the story, the structure of the labyrinth was so confusing that even Daedalus himself could barely get out of it once he had built it. The Minotaur lived in the labyrinth for a long period of time, and every year seven youngsters were sent to the labyrinth as food for

---

[*] Sigmund Freud. *El Chiste y su relación con el inconsciente. Capitulo: El chiste y las especies de lo cómico.* p. 228. Ed. Lectorum. México.

the monster. Finally, it was Theseus who successfully entered the labyrinth and killed the Minotaur, with the help of Ariadne, who gave him a ball of thread to retrace his steps. However, there have been other labyrinths, as Juan Eduardo Cirlot mentions in his *Dictionary of Symbols*: the labyrinth in Egypt at the Lake Moeris; the two on Crete: at Knossos and Gortyna; the Greek one on the island of Lemnos; and the Etruscan labyrinth in Clusium. Virgil also tells us that a labyrinth is drawn at the entrance to the cave of the Sibyl of Cumae. Some paths within a labyrinth are dead ends, and while going through them little by little the exit or the center of it is discovered. The labyrinth, being associated with the cave, leads us to think that the fact of going through it is an initiatory journey, where there are tests to pass, and each of them is an initiatory ordeal that we must face and recognize to appreciate its value. Thus, in those comings and goings that we make within the labyrinths, there is also an ascetic-mystical journey, since we focus on ourselves through complex paths and false exits. The individual who walks a labyrinth undergoes a spiritual death and resurrection. It is as if we were stripped of old clothes and only the manifestation of our pure and authentic being is allowed to remain.

The Spider as a Weaver of the Labyrinth

Marcel Brion tells us that "The comparison of the labyrinth with the spider's web is not exact," that "the spider's web is symmetrical and regular, while the very essence of the labyrinth is to circumscribe in the smallest possible space the most complex entanglement of paths and thus delay the departure of the traveler to the center to be reached."[†]

We can agree or not with the previous idea, whether the labyrinth of our LIFE is symmetrical or not; whether the

---

[†] Chevalier Jean. *Diccionario de Símbolos*. p.706. Ed. Herder

labyrinth of our LIFE (I capitalize the word life, since I refer to life in the full sense, encompassing all our previous and future incarnations in the multiverse and not just in this incarnation where we are) is circular, spiral, or pyramidal, etc. What we are interested in knowing here is that our labyrinth is not yet fully finished and is not symmetrical. For this reason, it is compared to the spider's web, a battered web, torn in some parts by weather conditions, attacks of other beings, etc. We, like the Spider, have built our own web, our own personal labyrinth in this incarnation and in many others, having had successes and failures, mistakes and good results. The thread that the Spider weaves from itself is the same that we weave when directing and leading our lives. We are our own weavers of our destiny and there is no one else. Just like the spider's web, which is made of rays and concentric circles, in our life there are warps and wefts, which are linked to our unconscious, to our center, to the beginning and origin of everything that is our Self.

Objective of This Work

Having pointed out the above, we can say that going through our labyrinth leads us to the interior of ourselves, to what is hidden by many masks, and where the greatest mystery is concealed - the deepest part of ourselves. Psychoanalytically speaking, this means the depths of unconscious, that (unique) center of ourselves that cannot be reached by consciousness, but can only be accessed if we dive into the depths of our unconscious, entering that crypt, the cave, where we reach illumination, personal epiphany. There, inside the crypt, we will rediscover the lost unity of our being, which is disintegrated, torn like a spider's web by unfinished desires, professional failures, love and marital disappointments, failed projects, etc. Brion mentions that "The more difficult our journey is, the more painful it is and the more and more tests, difficulties and obstacles we encounter, the more we will transform ourselves and the more we will transform our Self."[‡]

This transformation of the Self can be broken down into the passage from darkness to light, in the triumph of the spiritual over the material, intelligence over instinct, knowledge over blind violence - we ourselves are our own psychopomp. No one is going to come through our labyrinth for us. Besides, I don't think anyone would want to, do you?

Jean Chevalier in his *Dictionary of Symbols* mentions that for the Bambara in Mali, "the spider symbolizes a higher degree of initiation. Individuals who have reached the interiority and the realizing power of the intuitive and meditative man."[§] Well, like the Bambara in Mali, we will carry out this work with that intention. These workings consist of a series of rituals, one for each day, which must be completed entirely, that is, you must pass the tests of each day, reach the center and exit the labyrinth. If you do not leave the labyrinth, you run the risk of being trapped psychically, without reaching the previously stated objective.

Development of Rituals

The present work is carried out on six consecutive days. The first day is dedicated to the invocation of the Spider Goddess and asking her to guide us through our labyrinth. In the days that follow we will go through our personal labyrinth, understanding it as the labyrinth of our current incarnation, from the moment we were born until today. This series of rituals is connected with a psychoanalytic theme, that is, we will explore some key concepts of psychoanalysis as we go through the labyrinth, such as the Oedipus complex (men), the Electra complex (women), narcissism, etc. The purpose

---

[‡] Chevalier Jean. *Diccionario de Símbolos*. p.710. Ed. Herder
[§] Chevalier Jean. *Diccionario de Símbolos*. p.97. Ed. Herder

is to get to know ourselves better, just like the Bambara in Mali. I do not provide any explanations of these concepts here, because there is a wide network of information in libraries and on the Internet that can be researched for that. Likewise, these rituals must be completed in their entirety from the first day to the sixth day, because if we fail, our psyche may become trapped and left in suffering. They must be performed at twilight.

Items needed

- ❖ Sigil of Spider Goddess of the Labyrinth - painted in black color on a dark green background.
- ❖ One black candle and one green candle.
- ❖ Copal incense, rue, musk, benzoin.
- ❖ Bitter tea: wormwood, rosemary.
- ❖ It is recommended to listen to some tracks of the Nox Arcana's album *Grimm Tales* at the beginning of each session.

First Day
Invocation of the Spider Goddess of the Labyrinth

On the first day you need to perform the invocation to the Spider Goddess. For this reason, focus on a mantra to invite the Goddess. This mantra will be repeated at the beginning of each ritual. You will repeat it for as long as you want, until you are attuned to the Goddess. The labyrinth in the sigil is reversed because you are forcing yourself to think and feel in a non-linear way. Once you are ready with the preparations, you need to place the sigil of the Spider Labyrinth on the altar, flanked by two candles: one black (right) and one green (left). There you should also have the chalice with some bitter tasting tea or bitter drink, which does not affect your health, though. Start by breathing three times, and then begin to recite the invocation. When it is finished, raise the chalice and drink all the liquid in it, leaving nothing inside.

Sigil of the Goddess of Labyrinth

Mantra of the Spider Goddess of the Labyrinth:

Oh! Spider Goddess,
I ask you to help me navigate the labyrinth of my life,
take me to walk its paths and thus arrive
to the center of my life and to know what I should know

and to see what I should see.
So be it.

Close your eyes and whether sitting, lying down, or standing, imagine that it is night and you are in a forest. The wind feels cold, the branches of the trees look dark in the moonlight, and you can see that they are crooked branches. At your feet a path appears and you begin to follow it as you walk. Some branches rip your clothes as if they were doing it on purpose. You walk like this for a few minutes until in the distance you see a being dressed in a black tunic. You approach the figure, and you can see its face now. The person standing in front of you points you to the entrance of the labyrinth, but it is blocked by a stone. Then this mysterious being tells you that in order to enter you must offer our blood and smear it on the entrance of the door so that it opens on each of the following days. That said, you are told to return to the place where you started, and you do so, returning to the starting point. You open your eyes and thank the Spider Goddess for allowing you to carry out this ritual. Write down in your diary the experiences and dreams you had on this first day.

Second Day
The Trauma of Birth

On the second day you should proceed in the same way as on the first day: perform the invocation of the Spider Goddess and drink from her chalice filled with bitter tea of your choice. Once you are on the way to your labyrinth, visualize that you arrive at the entrance, where the same figure awaits you. You anoint the front of the door with your blood and it opens up. You immediately enter the labyrinth, visualizing it in a personal way, that is, your labyrinth will be different from others, because your life is also different. You start walking forward, without turning back at any time along the way. Take a good look at the walls as you are walking, because they reflect the way your life goes. Maybe they are not completely dark, maybe there are parts with light, you never know. You see places where there are shadows and beings that you do not know, false doors that lead to wrong decisions, mistakes, or those that lead to successes. You continue walking, looking for the entrance where it is written: "The Trauma of Birth." Once you find this entry, you enter, and inside you see a spider web which reflects your life. Anoint it with your blood and mentally ask yourself the question: "What is the vital event of my birth?" Gradually, you begin to visualize your own birth on the web and everything that was involved in making it happen, events that influenced and triggered it. Once you have seen everything in the web, leave the place, open your eyes, and thank the Spider Goddess for allowing you to perform this ritual. Write down in your diary the experiences and dreams you had on this day.

Third Day
Oedipus Complex - Electra Complex

On the third day proceed in the same way as before. Again, perform the invocation of the Spider Goddess and drink from her chalice filled with bitter tea. Then start where you left off the day before, going through the different paths of your labyrinth, this time looking for the entrance where it is written: "Oedipus Complex" or "Electra Complex." Observe what your labyrinth looks like - the dark and the bright parts. You will see holes with shadows and unknown beings, false doors that lead to wrong decisions. Once you reach the entrance, you enter and in the same way you see in front of you a great spider web that reflects your life. Anoint it with your own blood and say mentally: "My Electra complex or Oedipus complex, as the case may be." You will now observe the scenes of your childhood that refer to that period of your life. You will feel the love or desire towards your father or mother, which perhaps is not fully resolved from then. Take note of all this and leave the place. Open our eyes and thank the Spider Goddess for allowing you to perform this ritual. Write down in your diary the experiences and dreams you had on this day.

Fourth Day
Narcissism

On the fourth day proceed in the same way as before, i.e., start with the invocation of the Spider Goddess and drink from her chalice. Then start walking where you left off the day before, looking for the entrance where it is written: "*Narcissism and Self-esteem.*" Continue in the same way: enter the web, anoint it with your blood and ask yourself mentally: "What aspects of my narcissism block my development as a person? What makes me feel false and unloved? What makes up for what I lack?" Focus on the spider's web and see what has been hindering you, or what you lack to lead a better life. When you feel that you have received the answers to your questions, leave the place, and thank the Spider Goddess for allowing you to perform this ritual. Write down in your diary the experiences and dreams you had on this day.

Fifth Day
Repetitions

On the fifth day proceed in the same way as before. Again, perform the invocation of the Spider Goddess and drink from her chalice. Then start walking where you left off the day before, this time looking for the entrance where it is written: "Your Repetitions." Enter in the same way as before, anoint the spider's web with your blood and ask yourself mentally: "What do I constantly repeat and cannot find?" You will see the part of your past that escapes you and you cannot catch, that is, your traumas. You will observe scenes of your past that show the compulsive repetitions in your daily life. When you feel that you have received the answers to your questions, leave the labyrinth, and thank the Spider Goddess for allowing you to perform this ritual. Write down in your diary the experiences and dreams you had on this day.

Sixth Day
Encounter with the Goddess
Catharsis

On the last day you need to perform the invocation of the Spider Goddess, too. Do not drink from the chalice yet, though. Instead, look for the entrance to the center of the labyrinth first. When you find the center, enter it. Inside you will see the figure of an arachnid or a woman dressed in black. However she manifests, approach her and you will see that a poison is dripping from her mouth, falling in drops into the chalice that she carries in her hands. As you get closer, visualize that she offers you her chalice (which is a stone cup, black spiders coming out of it), which you take with your both hands. Thank her and drink it all, doing the same with your chalice on the altar. You will feel how your consciousness becomes altered, how your senses change and transform. You may also feel nauseous or dizzy, which is normal, since the essence of the Spider Goddess is in you. Once stabilized, thank her for allowing you to perform her rituals in this work and to get to know yourself better. Then leave the labyrinth. Write down in your diary the experiences and dreams you had on this last day.

The Gnosis and Alchemy of the Spider

Lucath

Major themes of the Spider Current are time, personal growth, building/constructing, strength, and wisdom. This is one of many reasons that the Spider Current often leads people into themselves and their pasts. This ritual series is aimed at doing just that: I intend this work to be theurgical with the aim of learning about or changing the Self. Before beginning, I encourage you to take a day or so to consider what you would like deeper clarity on in your life or what you'd like to change about yourself (unless you just instantly know). But you could adapt this series for a variety of other purposes, even just learning more about the Spider Current. So, *consider what you want.*

While each ritual is slightly different, I encourage you to do these rituals as minimally as possible in order to focus more on the dissociative aspects of trance in order to more easily commune with these energies. If you have or would like to use all the elements I describe, please do; however, do not feel limited to *have to* use any of them. These rituals are purposely minimal in accoutrement so go even more minimal if you'd like: spiders create webs from *their own energy*. But do all of the rituals in a darkened room when possible.

Ritual 1
Going Back into the Cave: Evoking the Spider Goddess

The Spider Goddess is a well-known spider entity for most Draconian Magickians. While she has many names and faces, she in many ways arguably represents a more primal, fierce version of the Greek goddess Arachne, who as a mortal challenged the gods morally, creatively, and pragmatically. And that is what we're going to call on her for here and in subsequent rituals. Depending on who you ask, the Spider Goddess may or may not be related to Lilith or her current. Considering this theme while working with her, she showed me "a secret entrance" to her current through the Cave of Lilith (This ritual is an adaptation of the "Cave of Lilith" ritual found in *Qliphothic Meditations*). And while this may be seen as evidence by some that Lilith and Arachne are connected, remember that you can connect with nearly the entire Qliphoth through the Cave of Lilith. So, are they?

Ritual

Pour a small glass of red wine (or replacement). Light a red candle (left) and a black candle (right). Place the sigil of the Spider Goddess between the candles in front of you. Anoint the sigil with your blood and put a few drops on your ritual dagger as well. Use the blade to draw the glyph of the trident in the air above the altar. Focus on the temple sigil while feeling the energies flowing through you, connecting you to the Current of the Dragon.

Then draw a trident with wormwood oil on your third eye and focus your attention on the sigil of the Spider Goddess.

As you stare at the sigil, contemplate your intended goal for this ritual: what in your life would you like more clarity on? What would you like to change about yourself? What insights would you like about or from the Spider Current? Let yourself get swept up in this thought process, using it as the meditative trance for the ritual. When you believe you've clearly conceptualized this desire and will it fully, offer the sigil blood, and burn any incense or other offerings you would like. Watch as the sigil begins to open up, maybe becoming a toxic green color. Then, raise the glass of wine and state that this glass of wine represents her poison and is an embodiment of anything she offers you in the ritual to bring her lessons to this plane. Stare at the sigil again until you feel you have a good connection with the Spider Goddess. Snuff or blow out the candles leaving yourself in total darkness.

See yourself on the path to Lilith's Cave: a tight path through a dark forest. As you traverse the path, follow the spiders taking the same path through the dark woods into the cave. In the main chamber, the eleven pointed star is lit up with fire, but the spiders follow the left wall into a darkened corner with a small, previously invisible circular staircase. Follow the spiders into the shadows and down the staircase. The stairs lead to an ornate throne room where a woman or spider or spider-woman sits upon a large throne in a neon green dress. As you approach, all eyes turn to you. Clearly state your desire and ask for her help acquiring it and the power to utilize, transmute, or overcome anything painful or hindering that comes up in the process. Listen to her answer. Ask her any follow-up questions you'd like. Eventually, she will hand you a cup of poison. Drink it and notice how it buzzes and burns throughout your body, eventually "killing you." Once the pathworking is finished, hold up the glass of wine and thank the Spider Goddess for her gnosis and help. See the wine as a representation of the poison she gave you. Drink it.

Ritual 2
Meeting the Fates and the Hidden Sister

In this ritual, we will work with the Greek version of the Fates (*Moirae*) and their hidden sister. While having ancillaries in other traditions (most notably the *Nornir*), the *Moirae* are described as the weaver (*Clotho*), alloter/measurer (*Lachesis*), and cutter (*Atropos*). The three sisters represent the "destiny" human beings are unable to escape. Yet, as Orryelle Defenestrate-Bascule points out in *Time, Fate, and Spider Magic*, if you overlap the traditional symbol for the three sisters and the traditional symbol for the crossroads, it leaves open a space for a third symbol and sister - one facing the other three as if at the crossroads and one that represents the dark phase of the moon. They write, "The dark phase of the moon is thus a ' c r a c k ' between the worlds, a potent time - or perhaps even space beyond time - for seeding new realities at the end of a cycle and the beginning of a new one (sic)" (63-4). Each of the sisters have something interesting to express, but together with the fourth sister show you a larger, more holistic version of the cycle of fate and destiny and may teach you a way to gain more control over it. If possible, do this ritual on a new moon.

Ritual

Light a red candle (left) and a black candle (right). Place the sigil of the Fates between the candles in front of you. Defocus your eyes and look at the sigil while you contemplate your desire and what the Spider Goddess told you yesterday. Consider how you'd like the Moirae to help you with that.

Draw a crescent moon in your blood on the sigil. Defocus your eyes and look at the sigil until you feel or see it open. Snuff or blow out the candles.

Qliphothic breathe** until you are in total darkness. Visualize the sigil and notice as it morphs into the three Moirae: Clotho (the spinner), Lachesis (the allotter), and Atropos (the inflexible). Ask each of them in turn about your life. For example: Why was it spun this way? Are there any hidden aspects that aren't being seen or expressed? Is anything missing? How long is it? Can you alter your death date? Can you and should you want to escape the reincarnation cycle?

When the Moirae have nothing left to tell you, thank them. Turn around. There is a staircase that goes into the ground. Descend the staircase, finding yourself in front of a door guarded by Cerberus. The dog allows you to enter the door. On the other side, there is a small room with a small circular pool of blood surrounded with three mirrors. Stand in the blood and look in the mirrors. The one in front of you shows you as a middle aged woman. The one to the left, a young woman. The one to the right, an old woman. Use the blood to draw a crescent moon on one of the mirrors and watch as the woman in that mirror turns into you. Ask them to tell you how the dark moon "crack" can help you influence your fate and thank them for their help doing that.

** Qliphothic breathing is a meditation where as your physical body breathes in air, you experience yourself breathing out light; as your physical body breathes out CO_2, feel and see yourself breathe in darkness. It's included in *Draconian Ritual Book.*

Sigil #1 The Fates & Hidden Sister:

Ritual 3
Māyā's Web of Illusions

In Vedic mythology, Māyā has a rather complicated role depending on context and philosophical positions. Her name means unreality or illusion and she is often thought of as the phenomenal world, more specifically as that aspect that constantly changes and obfuscates and hides the absolute. In other words, because the world is phenomenal (experienced through our senses), we experience the world in, through, and as illusion because we only see what our senses show us, and they may show us different things. Māyā is this illusion specifically. But in a certain sense, this means that the phenomenal world of "illusions" is also the divine mother because we live phenomenal lives that may allow us to approach the absolute within the illusion, we can see beyond it. So, in this way, Māyā is also the way into truth. She is sometimes written of as the weaver or spider, but sometimes this designation is given to Brahman. Regardless, for our purposes here, she controls the ever evolving phenomenal world, the illusion of largely being trapped within our own perception, and the ability to see through the illusion. Here we are petitioning her to help us to see through and overcome the illusions in our own life.

Ritual

Light enough candles to illuminate the sigil. Burn enough incense to make it a little hazy in the room. Offer the sigil blood if you would like. As you sit, stare at the sigil and contemplate your desire. Rock yourself in circles one way, then the other, then the other, then the other until you feel a little disoriented. Blow out the candles and see yourself floating in darkness, but feeling your body sinking more and more with each passing moment like you were being pulled down by some slow gravity. Notice that as you go deeper and deeper into the abyss, your body begins to feel incredibly heavy, but your mind feels lighter and lighter and more active. As your mind begins to float away from your body, you notice your body keeps floating down, feeling heavier and heavier. Float up and away up and away until you find yourself in a bright, white area covered with a massive spider web.

A woman with beautiful golden jewelry beckons you toward her. As you approach, she disappears and reappears ahead of you, again beckoning you forward. As you walk forward, you find yourself stuck in the web. The woman appears in front of you and snaps her fingers in front of your forehead. As she does, you see some of the illusions in your life. Some may have a flood or floods of gnosis here, others may only have a little or just the beginning. Regardless, thank her for her blessings even if you hope(d) for more. Ask her to help you in overcoming these illusions and ask if she has anything else to teach you. End the ritual naturally.

Sigil #2 Web of Māyā:

Ritual 4
Loom of Arachne

Arachne was a human woman that excelled in weaving. In the writing of Ovid, she is said to have challenged Athena to a weaving competition. Athena weaves of times that mortals were punished for challenging the gods and Arachne weaves a more beautiful tapestry than Athena detailing the times that the gods misled and abused humans, particularly how Zeus abused women. Athena, angered that she was bested by a blasphemer, hits Arachne on the head three times and destroys the woman's work. Arachne hangs herself and Athena turns her and her descendants into spiders using Hecate's herb. She encourages us to ask several things, but mainly what is my blasphemous hubris? Where do I excel beyond the gods? Where am I holding myself back to appease others? Use her energy to explore themes like this.

Ritual

Same basic setup as ritual one: red and black candle, draw a wormwood oil trident on your third eye, etc. Qliphothic breathe yourself into a deep level of darkness. Focus your attention on the Arachne/Spider Goddess sigil. Consider your desire and how Arachne's energy can help you. Offer it blood. Stare at it until it "opens." Snuff the candles.

See the sigil in your mind's eye expand until it's so large that it becomes one color. This color fades into you weaving an epic tapestry of the wrongdoings of the gods and those in power. Watch as your hands move and make a beautiful tapestry. While you're weaving, a spider crawls up your body and bites your neck. You feel a little faint and woozy and have to stop weaving. After a few moments, the feeling passes and your hands begin to weave a story that's relevant to you... When the ritual naturally fades, thank Arachne for her lessons and close the ritual.

Ritual 5
The Wisdom of Anansi

Anansi is an interesting being in the Spider Current because he is a male trickster. While he originally comes from Ashanti folktales, because of the slave trade, his stories have been told with different masks. So, people from the Americas may recognize him as Aunt Nancy or Br'er Rabbit. In a famous folktale, Anansi, a very clever spider wishes he were wiser. So, he takes a gourd and goes around town asking everyone for their wisdom (or stealing it depending on the story). Once he has all he can carry, he heads home, but he cannot figure out how to climb the tree to his home with only 6 legs while holding the gourd with the other two. His young son tells him to tie it to his back and he realizes that even though he has all the wisdom, he *still* needed the wisdom of a child. So, he decides wisdom is best when shared. Like Anansi, we have collected wisdom (about ourselves) and now it's time for it to be shared throughout our lives.

Ritual

Light enough candles to light up the room well enough that you can move if you would like to. Focus your attention on your desire and how you'd like Anansi to help with that. Offer the sigil blood and incense if you'd like, but it's optional here. Stare at the sigil until you feel yourself making a connection to him. Offer him a dance (preferably a traditional Afro-Caribbean one) while contemplating his folktale(s) or create a whimsical, entertaining chant or invocation off the cuff. (Do the best you can.) See the sigil in your mind's eye expand into a giant tree Anansi sits atop of. He has his gourd of wisdom. Tell him the wisest thing you have learned in this process or in your life. If he accepts this into his gourd, ask him to share the accrued wisdom with *all of you* and to add any additional wisdom he would like to add over the next 30-60 days. When the ritual naturally fades, thank Anansi for the wisdom and close the ritual.

Sigil #3 Anansi:

Arachne as a Zodiac Sign

Asenath Mason

I have decided to write this article because there is very little information on this subject. The book by James Vogh *Arachne Rising: The Search for the Thirteenth Sign of the Zodiac* was published over four decades ago and has not been rereleased since then. Perhaps there is not enough interest in his ideas among modern astrologers. It is, however, relevant for the study of Arachne and her manifestations in the history of Western esotericism, and I believe the information included in the book may still be of interest to a practitioner working with the Spider Goddess. For this reason, in this article I will present the ideas included in Vogh's book, and let the reader decide if it is interesting enough to pursue further.

The idea of thirteen zodiac signs instead of the popular twelve ones is not something new. Even if you have not heard about Arachne being the thirteenth one, you might have heard of Ophiuchus, which is another popular candidate for this position. Both, however, are still controversial and not always recognized or acknowledged by astrologers. According to Vogh, the reason for it may be the negative reputation of the number thirteen. Let us see what exactly this means. Thirteen is an ambiguous number, indeed. I am sure you have heard that Friday the 13th is generally an unlucky day, that some hotels do not have the 13th floors or rooms with this number, and generally, thirteen seems to bring forth a lot of negative associations. In the tarot, it is the number of the Death Atu, which is the most feared card in the entire deck. In occultism, thirteen is associated with death and rebirth, change and a new beginning after the end. It is a number that distorts the world order and disturbs the balance in the universe. For example, there are twelve months in a year, the twelve days of Christmas, the twelve apostles in the Christian tradition, etc. Adding the thirteenth one is believed to bring back luck, just like the presence of Judas at the Last Supper, who was the thirteenth to sit at the table and later betrayed Jesus. Some would say, however, that the dreadful reputation of thirteen is due to it being a female number. While there are twelve months in the calendar, there are thirteen lunar cycles, which is connected to the increased influence of the feminine currents during the thirteenth one. In ancient cultures, this number represented the menstrual cycles in a year ($13 \times 28 = 364$ days), and it was often believed to be the gateway to the mysteries of the Divine Feminine. Vogh observes that thirteen is related to irrational dreams, subconscious fears and desires. Therefore, the thirteenth zodiac sign is, in a natural way, the sign of "pure psychic force."

The number thirteen is also ascribed to Arachne in the Draconian/Typhonian Tradition. We encounter references to her gnosis in the writings of such authors as Michael Bertiaux or Kenneth Grant, and I have found many correlations between this number and certain aspects of her current through my own work with the Necronomicon and inter-dimensional gateways. According to Vogh, her astrological influence lasts 29 days, and during this time, as it is observed by Grant, the psychic transmissions from extraterrestrial dimensions are particularly intense. Grant further explains that the rays of the days interlaced with the rays of the nights form a web of fifty-eight (29x2) threads. In *Outside the Circles of Time*, he observes that the number twenty-nine concentrates to eleven, the number of the Qliphoth, and the number fifty-eight concentrates the power or *shakti* of thirteen, the red star of the lunar current. In my own work with the Spider Goddess I have found a formula of thirteen gates through which her powers may be explained from the perspective of the Draconian/Ophidian magic, which is described in detail in my book *Necronomicon Gnosis*. She is also worked with extensively in my grimoire *Tunnels of Set*, where the work with her is focused on the Qliphothic aspects of her current and the magic of the Void. If you are interested in the Draconian/Typhonian perspective on Arachne, of special interest is also the text called *Book of the Spider (OKBISh)*, which was channeled by members of New Isis Lodge (1955-62) and included in Grant's *The Ninth Arch*.

In Vogh's opinion, we can find evidence for the thirteenth sign already in ancient times, where it is mentioned, or at least hinted at, in various myths, poems, artifacts, drawings, and writings. According to him, it was "lost" because it was considered as "dangerous" knowledge. He also observes that the zodiac was not always composed of twelve signs at all. For instance, the early Babylonians had eighteen signs, the Egyptian zodiac included thirty-six, the Aztec twenty, and the Chinese once divided the circle of the year into four signs, which were the Green Dragon, the White Tiger, the Red Quail, and the Black Tortoise. There are zodiacs with 8, 16, or 20 divisions, depending on the culture and the historical context in which these divisions appeared. Twelve is a number often prevailing in the West, but it is not the only one in relation to the zodiac. Vogh provides several examples on what this division looked like in ancient times in various civilizations. For instance, he writes about the Aztecs and their interpretation of this number, observing that they "divided the day into thirteen hours, each ruled by a divinity, and they instituted a week of thirteen days." Another division he refers to is the Druid calendar of thirteen months of twenty-eight days each, being a lunar calendar, instead of the solar-based Western division. Still another is the one depicted by inscriptions upon the plain at Nazca, Peru. Vogh observes that one of the figures included there is a spider, which, together with the other animals, represents constellations, while the entire set of inscriptions is said to be the map of the heavens. He also claims that all calendar-making civilizations associated the number thirteen with fate.

Arachne as the Spider Goddess is a ruler of fate as well, as you may read in other articles in this anthology. This is also the role she is worked with in the Temple of Ascending Flame, apart from her function of the ruling force of the Tunnels of Set. The association of the spider symbolism with fate is an old idea, encountered in many mythologies worldwide. The Greek Arachne was a talented weaver, who could depict anything with her thread. The same quality is found in the mystical meaning of the spider - it is the weaver of the web that represents the pathways of our life - our choices, actions and decisions. All of them are interconnected and one always affects the others. By changing one small thing in our life, we can change our entire future. The same idea is used to explain destiny - by manipulating the threads in the Web of Arachne we can change the course of our life and alter our fate. For this reason, the spider has been associated with fate for a long time. It is enough to look at the number of spider deities encountered worldwide, such as the Sumerian Uttu, the African Anansi, the Native American depictions of the Spider Grandmother, etc. Many of them are figures whose actions alter destinies and introduce a change in the world.

Another example of a mythological figure connected with the symbolism of the spider is the Greek Ariadne. In the myth, she gifts Theseus, who she fell in love with, a ball of thread to help him find his way in the labyrinth of the Minotaur. Thanks to her gift he does not get lost, like the other adventurers who tried to kill the monster, and manages to get out of the labyrinth safely. Vogh interprets this myth in metaphorical terms, claiming that the gift of Ariadne was some kind of guidance that helped Theseus navigate through "the labyrinth of his own unconscious," which further emphasizes the connection between the spider thread and the psychic abilities of an individual. According to Vogh, Ariadne and Arachne can be seen as the same figure, both being the names for the Spider Goddess.

An interesting analysis presented by Vogh is definitely the list of correspondences between the motifs on Arachne's tapestry and the zodiac signs. In the book, they are presented as follows:

1) Jupiter as a bull seduces Europa (Taurus).
2) Jupiter pursues Asterie (?)
3) Jupiter seduces Leda, who bears him twins (Gemini).
4) Neptune is disguised as a river god (Cancer).
5) Phoebus is dressed in a lion's skin (Leo).
6) Erigone, the virgin (Virgo).
7) Danae weighs gold in her lap (Libra).
8) Jupiter as a spotted snake (Scorpio).
9) Birth of the centaur, Chiron (Sagittarius).
10) Neptune, the sea god, disguised as a ram (Capricornus).
11) Jupiter seduces the daughter of the river (Aquarius).
12) Neptune disguised as a dolphin (Pisces).
13) Apollo disguised as a herdsman (Aires).

Vogh refers to the Ovid's version of the myth, so instead of the Greek names, we have the Roman Jupiter and other mythological figures of ancient Rome, but the idea is the same as in the Greek myth of Arachne. He explains that the thirteenth image, which is not associated with any zodiac sign (#2: Jupiter pursues Asterie), in fact refers to Arachne, who is here disguised as Asterie ("of the starry sky"). The validity of this can be debated, though, as there is actually a mythological figure named "Asteria," to which this depiction may refer. Asteria ("the starry one") was a Titaness, known for being pursued by Zeus, who lusted for her as she was of a great beauty. In the myth, to escape his advances, she transformed herself into a bird, and then into a wandering island. Asteria is also known to be the wife of the Titan Perses and the mother of Hecate, another mythological figure associated with choices, transformation, and altering the destiny by means of witchcraft and "forbidden" magic.

In Vogh's theory, there is a lot about the spider being a symbol of psychic abilities and its connection to the unconscious. He ascribes to it the powers of imagination, natural connection to magic, inventiveness, brilliance, cleverness, etc. The same qualities he ascribes to those who were born at the time when, according to him, the influence of the thirteenth zodiac sign is the strongest. He also observes that the greatest inventions of mankind were connected with the spider symbolism, like the secret of making fire. In his view, even the myth of Prometheus bringing fire from the heavens to the earth can be associated with the spider gnosis. This is because the name of Prometheus may be related to the Sanskrit word *pramantha,* which means "fire-wheel," with the wheel being the masculine equivalent to the feminine spindle. It is also related to the concept of a spiral with a center - the motif found in many graphic depictions all over the world. The web, the spindle, the wheel, the labyrinth - are all symbols of a mystery that is to be unraveled, explored, and penetrated in order to bring forth illumination and wisdom. It is also a symbol of both creation and destruction, as the spider builds and destroys its web continuously, which may be viewed as a metaphor for the human life - we continuously undergo changes and transitions, rites of passages and moments of self-sacrifice. For this reason, Vogh makes a claim that the most common form of Arachne is the wheel of four spokes, also known as the Celtic cross. In modern times, he observes, this is represented by the astrological symbol for Earth: ⊕ He justifies this claim by saying that Earth is the only planet never shown on horoscopes, the true reason for it being that it is, in fact, nothing else than the original symbol for Arachne, the Spider. While this claim may be debated as well, I was personally struck by this idea because the very first sigil for the Spider Goddess which I received in my work with her was a simple image built around a cross. It was used for a while in the Temple of Ascending Flame before it got replaced by a more complex sigil, reflecting the Arachnean and Ophidian nature of the goddess. I still use it sometimes in my own work, although by now I have received many other symbols for the Spider Goddess, of which the primary is shared here, on page 36.

Let us now get to the most interesting part, i.e., when exactly we can expect to see "Arachne rising." According to Vogh, the Sun enters the sign of the Spider on May 16th and leaves it on June 13th. At the moment of writing this article, it is the second half of May, which would indicate the greatest influence of the Spider Goddess in the entire year. Is it really so? I personally believe that such influence depends on many more factors. In my own practice, I have found autumn and winter to be a better time to work with the Spider Goddess, who is a very dark and fearsome mask of the Dark Mother, the Goddess of the Qliphoth. Her energies are dissolving, and she injects her venom into the consciousness of the practitioner to transform it from within. This comes with a lot of introspection, self-reflection, and insights into our life, magical path, and existence in general. For me personally, the long winter evenings are a better time for such work, which in a lot of ways belongs to the domain of shadow magic. When all life in nature ceases and the veil between the realms of the living and the dead is thin, it is easier and more natural for me to access the personal underworld and work with the subconscious material than it is now, when sun is high, the nature is fully awakened after the winter, and everything around is filled with life and vitality. All depends on a practitioner, though, and perhaps the influence of Arachne, the Spider, is stronger at the moment on the southern hemisphere.

Coming back to Vogh's theories, people born under the sign of the Spider, or "the Araneans," have a greater chance of being psychic than those born under any other sign, and are always "special" in some way. To prove his point, he mentions a number of famous people, who were poets, artists, and talented individuals in general, such as Walt Whitman, W.B. Yeats, Arthur Conan Doyle, Allen Ginsberg, Henry Bulwer-Lytton, and many others. He provides a list of people involved in music, film, politics, etc., including names such as F.A. Mesmer, Bertrand Russell, Norman Vincent Peale, or even Cagliostro. Then he examines the life of a few chosen figures to prove that they were influenced by the Spider. I am not going to include those explorations here, and if you are interested, you can read about it all in the book itself. Of course, this is a debatable claim as well, as we can find famous and talented people in all zodiac signs, and saying that only those born under the Spider are psychic and magically gifted is a highly controversial statement.

Another analysis provided by Vogh is connected with the concept of the Moon in Arachne, or the Spider ascendant. In astrology, these three things: the Sun, the Moon, and the rising sign, are the most important features of a birth chart. The spider itself is believed to be a lunar animal. The phases of the moon, with its growing and waning periods, are symbolic of creation and destruction, death and rebirth, just like the spider continuously weaving and destroying its web. To determine whether the Moon was in Arachne during the time of a person's birth, it is necessary to convert their birth chart according to the instructions provided in the book. Such a conversion, according to the author, transforms an ordinary birth chart into a "psychic horoscope," giving a better insight into the person's psychic powers, instead of merely focusing on the particular aspects of their life. Again, for the actual procedure, please refer to the book, where it is explained step by step, and seems fairly easy, even if you do not have anything to do with astrology.

Vogh also provides an overview of the particular planets in relation to the Spider. And so, Mercury in Arachne (☿⊕) governs speed, logic, sight, and quick-witted understanding. Venus in Arachne (♀⊕) presides over peace and harmony in love and relationships. Mars in Arachne (♂⊕) governs courage, force, physical strength, boldness, and ambition. People born under its influence are natural leaders, inventors, and possess a certain amount of mechanical and engineering talent. Those having Jupiter in Arachne (♃⊕) are characterized by cheerfulness, optimism and the "jovial" traits, as well as logic and determination. They tend to be honest, sociable, confident, and expansive. People with Saturn in Arachne (♄⊕) are cautious, slow-moving, conservative, melancholic, prone to depression and pessimism, and "Saturnine" in general. Uranus in Arachne (♅⊕) presides over science, astrology, magnetism, electricity, and unexpected events. Its influence is psychic and in relation to the Spider, it is doubly powerful. According to Vogh, people born with this position of Uranus demonstrate amazing psychic abilities. If you have Neptune and Pluto in Arachne (♆⊕, ♇⊕), you are magically talented as well. These are the planets of occult powers, and in combination with the psychic

Arachne, they have a great influence on the psychic abilities of a person, enhancing such powers as clairvoyance, telepathy, healing, and psychometry. Finally, the author also discusses the lunar nodes in Arachne (☊⊕, ☋⊕), which affect the psychic abilities as well, ruling over natural talents and the tendency to clairvoyance and prophesy.

The accuracy of these theories has been questioned many times and does not seem popular in modern astrology, as we rarely see any references to the "Spider sign" in any zodiac. I have found these ideas fascinating, not because I put much faith in astrology, which has never been part of my personal path, but because they give further insight into the nature of the Spider Goddess. In the same way I see the astrological concept of the "Black Moon Lilith," which has absolutely nothing to do with Lilith as a mythological figure, but is often discussed in relation to her in many modern sources. I see these theories, however, as relevant to the study of the Spider Current, which in today's world is stronger than ever before. Therefore, grab the book, convert your chart, and see if you were born with the natural "spider" abilities. If not, do not worry - in magic a lot can be trained, exercised, polished, and learned from the scratch, and you do not need to be a "natural Aranean" to work with the Spider Goddess. She is everywhere, and it is enough to reach out and open yourself to her influence to let her transform you through her deadly venom and her life-giving essence.

Contributors

Asenath Mason is a writer and artist. author of many books and essays on esoteric, religious and mythological subjects, with a particular focus on the Left Hand Path philosophy, Luciferian Spirituality and Draconian Tradition. Active practitioner of Occult Arts and teacher offering personal consultations and initiations into the Draconian Current. Founder and coordinator of the Temple of Ascending Flame. Co-author and editor of a number of anthologies and occult magazines. She is also a varied artist, working with digital media, and themes of her artwork include various gothic, fantasy and esoteric concepts.
Contact & more information: **www.asenathmason.com**

Charlie Demos - Emerging from the magickal muddy chaos that is the beautiful city of New Orleans, Charlie Demos is a Black Magician and initiate of the Temple of Ascending Flame. He works as a Psychic Medium offering divination, spiritual guidance, private lessons, and spell work on a case by case basis. Charlie is an initiated priest of Vodou and Palo Mayombe as well as a freelance writer, spoken word artist, musician and filmmaker.
If you would like to connect please email:
qliphothicreflection11@gmail.com

Darío G. - from Querétaro, México, with more than ten years in Paganism, initiate of several traditions, such as Wicca Alexandrina in France (Cauldron of Rebirth) or paganism in México. Practitioner of magic - RHP - and dedicated to the Golden Circle

in Spain. Initiate and enthusiastic member of the Temple of Ascending Flame. Philosopher and psychoanalyst.
Contact information: **israel.hernandez14@gmail.com**

David Weaver is a Draconian Magickian, occultist, professional channeler, energy worker, writer and member of the Temple of Ascending Flame located in the United States. He has "officially" been walking the left hand path of spirituality since 2016; although, he has been drawing dragons, battlefields and pentagrams ever since he could hold a pencil to paper. He is also a lifelong martial artist, musician and metal head (mostly black and death metal these days). He loves Halloween and is interested in all things dark and macabre. If you would like to get in touch with him, send him a message, give feedback or find out more about his services, you may email him at:
93Agape93@Tutanota.com.

Denerah Erzebet is the author of *The Draconian Trilogy* and *Nature's Stronghold.* As a classical composer, Denerah works towards honoring a Traditional worldview, inspired in equal parts by the genius of Richard Wagner and the insights of Julius Evola. Denerah Erzebet can be contacted at the following profile page:
https://www.scoreexchange.com/profiles/denerahbathory

Edgar Kerval is an author and musician coming from Colombia, South America. He has been working through more than 20 years with diverse paths of sorcery. He focuses on elements regarding saturnian gnosis dealing with death entities from diverse pantheons. Also, he works on many ritual ambient musical projects such as EMME YA, THE RED PATH, ARCHAIC:, among others. He has his own small publishing house called SIRIUS LIMITED ESOTERICA, in which he publishes some of his works and the books of other well-known authors. He has participated in II and III International Left Hand Path Consortium in Atlanta and St Louis respectively. He has released many books and participated in several anthologies.
www.emmeya111.bandcamp.com
siriuslimitedesoterica.blogspot.com

Keona Kai'Nathera Darkfang is a Satanic Daemonlatress whose practices include necromancy, blood Magick, oracle workings, herbology, and Vodou. She is a HPS with the Brotherhood of Satan, a member of Temple of Ascending Flame, and helps run the Daughters of Lilith, a woman only online occult study group with her Coven sisters on Facebook. You can contact her on her website **www.queensenigma.com**, on YouTube under Serenity Keona, and on IG as keonakainathera. You can also reach her at **tribalsqueen@gmail.com**

Lucath has been fascinated with magick since coming across Crowley's auto-hagiography in a library as a preteen. Though he's explored many traditions (even Wicca), he's most influenced by the chaos tradition and the pragmatism that comes from a minimalist and mostly secret solo practice. His magickal work focuses strongly on theurgy and ever-ascending "a pile of dead selves" to higher evolutions of self. Much of his work is with the divine feminine and the archetypes of desire, creation, birth, evolution, abortion, destruction, and death and how that relates to personal evolution. A student of western philosophy, the occult, LBM, and an avid reality tunneler, he revels in being on a Faustian quest beginning with trying to memorize the dictionary before starting school. "The mind is its own place, and in itself can make a heaven of hell, a hell of heaven" - John Milton.
Email: **fraterlucath@gmail.com**

Recommended Reading

Kenneth Grant: Typhonian Trilogies 1-9, in chronological order: *The Magical Revival, Aleister Crowley and the Hidden God, Cults of the Shadow, Nightside of Eden, Outside the Circles of Time, Hecate's Fountain, Outer Gateways, Beyond the Mauve Zone, and Ninth Arch.*

Edgar Kerval: *Lil Az H Az Lil: The Grimoire of the Arachnean Goddess*

Orryelle Defenestrate-Bascule: *Time, Fate and Spider Magic*

James Vogh: *Arachne Rising: The Search for the Thirteenth Sign of the Zodiac*

Asenath Mason: *Necronomicon Gnosis: A Practical Introduction*

Asenath Mason: *Tunnels of Set*

Temple of Ascending Flame

Temple of Ascending Flame is a platform for individuals around the world who want to share certain aspects of their work with the Draconian current with other adepts of the path and for those who simply need guidance into Draconian self-initiatory magic. It is both for newcomers who make their first steps on the Path of the Dragon and for experienced individuals who wish to progress on the Left Hand Path. We are not a "magical order." We do not charge fees for membership and our work is not based on any hierarchies. There are no restrictions on participation in our open projects, and in our inner work we welcome all who are capable of receiving and channeling the Gnosis of the Dragon.

More information: **ascendingflame.com**
Contact: **info@ascendingflame.com**

OTHER ANTHOLOGIES

RITES OF LUCIFER

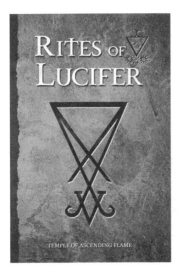

Lucifer is the archetype of the Adversary, initiator and guide on the Path of the Nightside. He is the fallen angel of Christian legends, the Devil of witches' Sabbats, one of primal Draconian Gods, Demon Prince of the Air, and Infernal Emperor of old grimoires. The purpose of this book is to delve into his initiatory role on the Draconian Path through chosen masks and manifestations which Lucifer has used over the ages to reveal his presence to mankind, bestowing his blessings on Initiates and scourging the ignorant. Essays and rituals included here explore both his bright and dark aspects, the face of the Light Bearer and the horned mask of the Devil.

Light and Darkness in Luciferian Gnosis by Asenath Mason - **The Light Bearer Ritual** by Temple of Ascending Flame - **Invocation of the Dark Initiator** by Temple of Ascending Flame - **The Mind of Lucifer** by Rev Bill Duvendack - **Purifying Fire (The Seed of Luciferian Gnosis)** by Edgar Kerval - **Lord of the Air** by Temple of Ascending Flame - **Lucifer - The Trickster** by Daemon Barzai - **The Shadow Companion** by Temple of Ascending Flame - **Holographic Luciferianism** by Rev Bill Duvendack - **The Adversarial Current of Lucifer** by Asenath Mason - **Invocation of the Adversary** by Temple of Ascending Flame - **Freedom through Death** by Cristian Velasco - **Emperor of Shadow and Light** by Pairika Eva Borowska - **The God of Witchcraft** by Temple of Ascending Flame - **The Infernal Spirit of Old Grimoires** by Temple of Ascending Flame - **Masks of Lucifer Ritual** by Rev Bill Duvendack

ISBN-13: 978-1505295092

TREE OF QLIPHOTH

Tree of Qliphoth is our third anthology, exploring the dark side of the Qabalistic Tree as a map of Draconian Initiation. In essays, rituals and other expressions of personal research and experience, magicians and initiates of the Draconian Tradition discuss the realms of the Nightside, teachings and gnosis of its dark denizens, as well as practical methods developed both within the Temple and through their individual work. Material included in this book will give the reader a foretaste of these forces and a glimpse of what you can expect while embarking on the self-initiatory journey through the labyrinths of the Dark Tree.

Lilith by Temple of Ascending Flame - **In the Cave of Lilith** by Asenath Mason - **Naamah** by S.TZΣ. Swan - Gates of Naamah by M King - **The Dark Tower** by Calia van de Reyn - **Gamaliel** by Temple of Ascending Flame - **Lilith and Samael** by Asenath Mason & Rev Bill Duvendack - **Samael** by Temple of Ascending Flame - **Invocation of Adrammelech** by Rev Bill Duvendack - **Poisoned Well** by Rev Bill Duvendack - **A'arab Zaraq** by Temple of Ascending Flame - **Invocation of the Dark Venus** by Asenath Mason - **Invocation of Baal** by Rev Bill Duvendack - **Niantiel Working** by Asenath Mason - **Thagirion** by Temple of Ascending Flame - **Invocation of Belphegor** by Asenath Mason - **Invocation of Sorath** by Asenath Mason - **Thagirion** by Pairika-Eva Borowska - **The Cave of Lafcursiax** by Edgar Kerval - **The Qabalism of Lucifer's Sigil** by Rev Bill Duvendack - **Golachab** by Temple of Ascending Flame - **Invocation of Asmodeus** by Christiane Kliemannel - **Invocation of the King of the Nine Hells** by Rev Bill Duvendack - **Nine Hells of Asmodeus** by Asenath Mason - **Gha'agsheblah** by Temple of Ascending Flame - **Invocation of Astaroth** by Christiane Kliemannel - **Seven Gates of the Underworld** by Asenath Mason - **The Abyss** by Temple of Ascending Flame - **Invocation of Choronzon** by Rev Bill Duvendack - **Invocation of Shugal** by Rev Bill Duvendack - **Invocation of the Beast of the Abyss** by Rev Bill Duvendack - **Opening the Gates of Choronzon to Sitra Ahra** by Zeis Araújo - Itzpapalotl by N.A:O - **Ritual of Babalon** by Asenath Mason - **Satariel** by Temple of Ascending Flame - **Invocation of Lucifuge** by Christiane Kliemannel - **Summoning of the Lord of the Night** by Rev Bill Duvendack - **The Spider and the Web of Fates** by Asenath Mason & Pairika-Eva Borowska - **Ghagiel** by Temple of Ascending Flame - **Invocation of Beelzebub** by Christiane Kliemannel - **Litany to the Lord of the Flies** by Rev Bill Duvendack - **Experiencing the Strength of Belial** by Mafra Lunanigra- **Thaumiel** by Temple of Ascending Flame - **Invocation of Moloch** by Christiane Kliemannel - **Invocation of Satan** by Christiane Kliemannel - **Thaumiel: The Mask of Arrogance as Freedom** by Leonard Dewar - **The Calling of the Twin God** by Rev Bill Duvendack - **The Two-Headed Dragon of Thaumiel** by Leonard Dewar - **Invocation of the Lord of Thaumiel** by Rev Bill Duvendack - **Three Hidden Chakras Working** by Christiane Kliemannel

ISBN-13: 978-1530016327

LILITH: DARK FEMININE ARCHETYPE

This anthology brings together essays, rituals, and unique artwork dedicated to the Queen of the Night and the Dark Goddess of the Qliphoth. Denied and rejected, worshipped and venerated, Lilith has been a part of the Western culture for ages. Viewed both as a beautiful seductress and a ruthless demon, she is the Serpent in the Garden of Eden, the first woman, and the primary initiatrix into the mysteries of the dark side of the Qabalistic Tree of Life. Her rites are the works of love and pain, sex and transgression, transcendence and immanence, for she exists at the roots of all desire of all humans past, present, and future. This archetype has never been fully grasped in its profundity and is constantly unfolding, challenging us to recognize our fears and passions and to transform them into tools of power. In this book you will find personal accounts of practitioners who ventured into the sacred and unholy garden of the Dark Queen of Sitra Ahra and returned transformed and empowered by her gnosis. Spells and invocations, dream magic and guided meditations, visions and stories of intimate encounters with Lilith - all this is contained in this unique anthology, written from the perspective of the Left Hand Path and the Draconian Tradition.

Asenath Mason: Introduction - Mike King: Sea of Ecstasy - Kai'Nathera: A Mother's Embrace - Asenath Mason & Rev Bill Duvendack: Fire and Lust - Martha Gray: Lilith and the Dual Nature of the Owl - Nemo.V: The Vase of Lilith - Katie Anderson: The Creative Fire: An Invocation to Lilith - Edgar Kerval: The Hidden Masks (A Lilith Exploration) - Rev Bill Duvendack: The Dark Feminine, a Man's Tale - Asenath Mason: The Unholy Grail - Mike King: Black Moon Lilith - Selene-Lilith: Selenic Face of Lilith - Greg Brown (aka Ahohlan): Journey into the Womb of Lilith - Alisa Jones: Lilith Queen of Tehiru Space - Asenath Mason: Lilith, Samael & Leviathan - Leonard Dewar: The Inconceivable Nature of Lilith - Lucien von Wolfe: Awakening the Vampire Within - Rev Bill Duvendack: The Mother of Abortions - Asenath Mason: The Mask of Medusa - Rev Bill Duvendack: Temple Astrological Correspondences

ISBN-13: 978-1979323260

SET: THE FURY OF EGYPT

As a self-created god, Set is a powerful archetype of the Adversary and an attractive model for a practitioner seeking initiation into mysteries of self-deification. Feared by the faint-hearted and worshipped by those who sought power, he has become a symbol of storm and change, movement and transformation, force and energy. His fiery nature represents lust and fury, which is the driving force on the path, and his Black Flame is the inner spark of Godhood that successively becomes the fiery pillar of ascent on the path of self-initiation. His forked knife cuts attachments to the surrounding world, liberating the initiate from bonds of slavery and mindless ignorance, and his scepter represents authority and power, showing us how to devour our gods and be the masters of our destiny. These portrayals of Set and many more are the subject of this anthology. Essays and poetry, portraits and sigil art, rituals and meditations – all these contribute to the portrayal of Set as a god that is still alive and active in modern times, perhaps even more than ever before. We will look into his origins, ancient myths and legends, and modern interpretations of his role on the Left Hand Path – all this written from the perspective of the Draconian Tradition.

Asenath Mason: Lord of Storm and Change - **Bill Duvendack:** Fragments and Figments - **Edgar Kerval:** Hymns of Adoration to Setekh - **Mimi Hazim:** My Journey into the Desert with Set - **Fra Diavolo:** The Role of Set in Western Occultism - **Fra Diavolo:** The Ritual of Set-Transformation - **Soror Sortela:** Breaking Boundaries: A Sexual Encounter with Set - **Asenath Mason:** The Flaming Star of Set - **Asenath Mason:** The Many Faces of Set - **Bill Duvendack:** Set: An Astrological Portrait - **Cătălina Deaconu:** Baptized in the Ecstasy of Poison - **Mimi Hazim:** The Gift of Demise - **Keona Kai'Nathera:** Walking with Set - **Asenath Mason:** The Lord of Fire - **V. Ghallego-Iglesias:** Rising up in the Middle of the Sandstorm - **Bill Duvendack:** The Gods of the Underworld - **Asenath Mason:** Set and Nephthys: Chaos and Void - SPECIAL CONTRIBUTION: **Michael W. Ford, Akhtya Dahak Azal'ucel, Sasutekhwoser V°, Priest of Heka, Priest of Set** - EGYPTIAN LEFT-HAND PATH MAGICK: The Neter Set and the Black Alchemy of the Ba and Ka

ISBN-13: 978-1798163535

HECATE: WITCHCRAFT, DEATH & NOCTURNAL MAGIC

Hecate is a goddess of witchcraft, lunar magic, and necromancy. She appears with torches in her hands, accompanied by howling dogs, serpents, and ghosts of the dead – terrifying retinue that roams the land under the cloak of the night. Her powers are many, and her cult involves both life and death – mystical transformation through the ultimate rite of passage and rebirth in the womb of the earth. She is benevolent and generous, both to nature and her worshippers, as well as ruthless and responsible for all nocturnal atrocities and rites of malefica. In ancient times she was believed to endow witches with the power over the forces of nature, reveal secrets of herbs and poisonous plants, and introduce her followers to mysteries of lycanthropy and shape-shifting. In the Draconian Tradition, she is the guardian of the mystical point of crossing, where all worlds, planes, and dimensions meet and intersect. Initiation into her path involves the descent into inner darkness, the personal "underworld," where knowledge of ourselves and our universe lies concealed, waiting to be rediscovered. She is the first initiatrix, the psychopomp, and the sentinel who meets the aspiring Initiate at the Crossroads of the Worlds, leading us into the Womb of the Dragon through the gateways of the Nightside. This anthology contains all those portrayals of Hecate and many more, introducing the reader to the magic and mythology of this mysterious goddess. Here you will find descriptions of personal gnosis revealed through the work of authors featured in this book, as well as references to her appearance in ancient lore and magic of old times. Like the other anthologies by the Temple of Ascending Flame, all this is written from the perspective of the Draconian Initiate, involving a modern approach suitable for the practitioner of the Left Hand Path

Asenath Mason: - Introduction - Mike Musoke: Hecate: The Goddess of Magic, Mysteries & Witchcraft - Asenath Mason: Three Faces of Hecate - Bill Duvendack: Hecate and Heqet - Denerah Erzebet: Spiritual Alchemy of the Triple Goddess - Keona Kai'Nathera: Hecate Workings - Asenath Mason: Hecate – Guide to the Underworld - Edgar Kerval: Atavistic Dream: The Great Goddess Rising - Bill Duvendack: An Anubis Hecate Cult - Selene-Lilith vel Belayla Rakoczy: Hecate and Mary at Polish Crossroads - Roberto Ruiz Blum: Hecate and Soul Alchemy - Asenath Mason:The Gatekeeper of Hell - Inara Cauldwell: Hecate, Prometheus and the First Mandrake - Satoriel Abraxas: Hecate's Rite of Passage into Timelessness - Asenath Mason: Draconian Sigil of Hecate - Noctulius Isaac: The Hall of Many Mirrors - Asenath Mason: Lycanthropy Rite - Bill Duvendack: Hecate Ritual: Walk with the Traveler - Asenath Mason: The Potion in the Cauldron & SPECIAL CONTRIBUTION: Jack Grayle – Hekate the Adversary

ISBN-13: 979-8718270600

Made in United States
Troutdale, OR
12/05/2024

25875963R00090